In the Darkness, a Match Was Lit

Miigwitch

You teachings
thus far have been
heart opening

Love
Darren

In the Darkness, a Match Was Lit

A Journey of Dying Before Living

Desnee Trevena

Strategic Book Publishing and Rights Co.

Strategic Book Publishing & Rights Co., LLC
USA
www.sbpra.net

For information about special discounts for bulk purchases, please contact Strategic Book Publishing and Rights Co. Special Sales, at bookorder@sbpra.net.

ISBN: 978-1-68235-775-0

ACKNOWLEDGMENTS

I want to thank everyone who has had a hand in loving me—you gave me your patience and support when it was difficult to do. Thank you for giving me a shot at life.

To my love, Adrian.

This certainly has been quite a ride we have been on in our sixteen years together. I can't express in words what your support, love, forgiveness and understanding, (even when you didn't understand what I was going through) has meant to me. You are my light in the dark. You are my laughter in my sadness. You allowed me to show myself to you–good and bad. You are the only man I have ever been sober with. And I wouldn't want it any other way. You and I started our healing journey together. Our years together haven't always been easy. But we fought for us—together. You are my right hand, my life-builder. Thank you for loving me when I didn't love myself.

I will always love you forever and a day.

To my editor, Michelle Clements.

Thank you for your assistance in helping me through the writing of my book. It was a difficult one for both of us. I appreciate you and I'm grateful that we were able to share this creation together. Your experience and talent is not unnoticed.

~ Desnee

Thank you.

Note from the author

The story you're about to read is one of fear and love. It's about pain and strength, but most of all, it's about acceptance and forgiveness. Read my story with unbiased eyes and an open heart. My story isn't unique unfortunately, but it is powerful, and it is mine to tell.

You are in for a roller coaster of a ride

– Desnee Trevena

Note from the editor

Dear Reader,

When I met Desnee in 2010, she was two years clean. I met her at a Cocaine Anonymous meeting. There was something I saw in her that I wanted, so I asked her to be my sponsor.

Unfortunately, at the time, I was clearly not ready to stay clean. When I came crawling back to the rooms, Desnee welcomed me, gave me money for cigarettes, and sent me in a cab to Women's Own Detox.

Our sponsorship did not work out because I refused to do the work. I just wasn't there yet. Over the years, Desnee has been supportive and brutally honest with me, which was something I lacked back then. She employed me to write a ten-week proposal for D. Gabriel Wellbriety in 2016.

Desnee is an amazing woman who has, as you will read in this book, battled and fought her way out of the darkest world of childhood trauma and subsequent addiction. She has reinvented herself and now is a counselor and a beacon for women and children who have been affected by childhood trauma.

Her friendship is something I treasure and this amazing strong woman inspires me every day. I am honored that she chose me to edit this remarkable work. I hope you enjoy this book and that you may learn from Desnee's experiences.

Michelle Clements

LETTERS TO MY CHILDREN

To my Children:

If I had one wish, it would be that each of your childhoods had been different.

I wish that I'd been healthy enough to care for you the way you needed and deserved to be.

I wish that our generational trauma had not affected you.

Along with my wish for the past, my hope for today, and the future, is that you have or will forgive me.

It's true that I am not responsible for what I saw growing up and how I was conditioned to handle the things that happened to me in my early years. However, I am fully responsible for how I live my life today and my healing journey. Always know that I will love you forever.

Love always, Mom

To my son, Cameron,

I could write a book on how much you mean to me.
    You are my baby and my first born.
    You're my love, my life, my everything. Baby boy, I wish I could love your pain away.
    I wish I could show you the gift that you are to those who love you. You are special and you deserve to be happy, and I wish that for you. You are my first greatest love and you will forever be.
    I dedicate this book to you to show you that you come from some powerful ancestors who helped me along my journey and are waiting to help you through yours. I love you son.

Love always, Mom

To my first born daughter, Chasity

The first time I looked into your eyes, I melted. You were my princess. A true gift from God, despite the ugliness that was happening in my life at that time. I would really like to say, I wish I could go back to when I gave birth to you or to when you were growing inside me, but I cannot. That time of my life was dismal indeed. You and Cameron were the only light in my otherwise dark world.

Maybe one day you'll believe that but, if not, that's okay too.

Please forgive me for not being the mother you needed. Forgive me for not being able to get clean and sober decades ago so I could have raised you. You may not understand this, but even if I did stop using, I still would have had a toxic mind. The toxicity would surely have trickled down to you. I never wanted that toxic soul for you.

I would never want you to be angry, resentful, and bitter like I was once.

I dedicate this book to you to show you my truth. To teach you that forgiveness is pure freedom from the bondage of self.

Despite the estrangement that you choose between us, I love you in a way you could never imagine.

I pray that you find peace.

Love always, Mom

To my mother's spirit, Celeste

My mother's child. You are spit out of my mommy's mouth.
Miss Glenda came back from the Spirit World through you.
Not to mention, when I grow up I wanna be just like you.
You have given me a place to exhale, a place to trust, and a place to feel true forgiveness.
You had to step into a role that wasn't yours at a very young age.
Please forgive me for making you grow up too fast. When I think of what you had to experience because I was in my addiction... The fact that I was asked to leave my home because I was using, just rips my heart apart.
You are truly my strength.
I dedicate this book to you because you are a part of my legacy. Your strength and courage to keep moving forward despite your obstacles is what drives me to want to be better and do better.
I'm here for you for as long as I'm breathing. I got you.
I love you so much. Love Mom.

To my child of strength, Cheyenne

Girl, you are one tough cookie. I think you have my "take-no-prisoners" side. But you're also my tender side. Those big brown eyes staring back at me instilled pure joy in my heart.

I think what hurts me the most in regard to you is that I could have lost you two times because of my drug use. Then you had to have some time away from me. I'm sorry that, when you needed me, I wasn't there nor could I have been. You're the fire under my feet, and because of you, I will never give up despite my challenges. Girl, I love you so much; I pray you never forget that.

I dedicate this book to you because you are my laughter, you are my beauty, and my number one, unofficial make-up and hair stylist. You and I have a relationship of freedom to express ourselves free of judgment. You've given me that and I thank you. I know you know this but let me say it again, whatever you need sugar, I got you.

Love always, Mom

To my baby boy, Curtis

You are my fire sign. I honestly believe that you chose me to be your mother, my baby boy, you were taken away from me for a brief moment at such a young age. I am happy that you really don't know or remember that. I was such a mess when you were born. I wasn't able to be the mother you needed. I tried, I really did, but I was just too sick at the time. Son, please forgive me. Until I leave this earth, I will give you every part of me. I will and do my best in teaching you independence and giving you my strength when you feel you have none. I'll hold your hand when you need me to, and even when you don't. I don't care how old you are, you will always be my baby. I love you; I can't even express that enough.

I dedicate this book to you in hopes that you will have an understanding of who your mommy was and who your mommy is. Also because every power I have in me, you also have in you. By reading this book, I hope you will find the tools you need to tap into your own power—to elevate yourself and bring you to where you need to be in this life. A king.

You already know without a doubt that I got you for life.
I will love you forever.

Love always, Mom

My Childhood

A Dedication To My Mommy Glenda

To know me, it is important to know the woman who gave birth to me. Her name was Glenda. Although she is with the Creator, my one hope is that she is smiling down on me, knowing that I have broken the cycle of addiction.

It was 1970 and my mom was arrested for solicitation. Her addiction rendered her powerless and wanting to escape, which is a feeling I know personally.

There was a story about her in the local newspaper, which included information about me, her young baby. Why they mentioned her child, I don't know. A year later, she gave birth to a son. Although I didn't know this then, my life would change forever.

I remember it being a sunny day. I was two years old.

Yes, I remembered that incident at that age.

Trauma will be remembered as long as you have memory. I also remember my maternal grandmother kicking my mother and me out of her house in the dead of winter. I wonder if these two are linked. Meaning was that incident, along with the other variables of my mommy's pain, what caused her to do what she was about to do? Just thinking about that choice makes me cry for both of us. Knowing what she was about to do, and every step closer, must've felt like walking one step closer to someone ripping her heart, soul, very being out. Also I found out recently that an aunt on my dad's side was caring for me for months because I was dropped off by my mom and dad—to watch me for a bit, but neither came back for me. Finally, Auntie told both or one of my parents (I'm not a hundred percent sure) to come and get me. She had grown so attached and knew she was going to be heartbroken when I was taken from her.

So many variables at my young age. Am I stalling? Could be but let me share this first: again—this memory is before my mom's heart was ripped from her, and my world changed forever.

I recall a time when my mommy, Glenda, had company and I was in my crib. I don't know why but a man came into the room and was trying to entertain me. He was wearing either my baby hat or my bib and he was dancing around. But how could it be mine? It would have been too small. Was it his size? I'll stop right there. I'll leave that image to your imagination.

Here is another:

I was with my nanny at her apartment on Augusta St., and she was yelling at the door. There was a man banging on the door. I know I was scared. I later found out that the other person outside the door was my paternal grandfather, Glen Harewood. I guess he needed to use the washroom and Nan wouldn't let him in so he literally shit in front of her door. Just like that. That's what I remember of that incident.

Speaking of Augusta, which was a street inside the Alexander Park Community Housing Projects, I always felt eerie in Nanny's building. Just getting off the bus at Queen Street to walk to the building made me anxious. But let's get back to the day I've been stalling about—the big day.

Chapter One

My biological father was nineteen and my mommy turned nineteen three weeks after I was born. I don't know if they were together when my mom gave birth. However, I have heard many stories about them being together, and how my mom betrayed my dad when he went to jail. Unfortunately neither was in a position to take care of me at that time. It's probably safe to say that a few people had a hand in caring for me for my first two years.

My brother and I have different fathers. We ended up being placed with my brother's biological father's family. My brother's father's Aunt E and Uncle L—who I came to know as Mom and Doc—raised us as their own.

My biological mother, Glenda, was a drug addict who was killed because of her addiction. I loved that woman with every ounce of my being and I am still very much traumatized by her loss. I was removed from her at the age of two and then I lost her permanently at the age of eleven. I love my dad and I miss him dearly. I had more time with my dad as a young child than I did with my mom because of her addiction. My maternal grandmother was a white Irish woman who, as far as I know, only dated black men. My grandfather was an amazing man who became a bad drunk, and who wound up homeless, begging for money to fund his alcoholism.

My grandmother was also an alcoholic. I acknowledge my grandmother's presence and, now that I'm older, I also acknowledge that something terrible must've happened to her to treat people the way that she did. She was a mean, nasty and loud woman. I blame her for my mother's death. She didn't actually kill my mother, but she certainly paved the way for my mother to become the person she was. She was always trying to run from her pain.

My grandmother gave my mother to her drunken friends for their sick, sexual entertainment at the age of ten. I challenge anybody to believe such a life isn't going to shape a person in a profound way. So not only did this sick woman destroy my mother, she also destroyed me and my children in the process.

I only remember seeing my grandfather one time and it was when my grandmother and grandfather were fighting. My grandfather was banging on my nanny's door but she wouldn't let him in. I don't remember seeing him at my mother's funeral. He may have very well been there, but I was never introduced to my maternal grandfather. Just one more blessing taken from me.

I was raised with the people I call my mom and dad (E and L) since I was two years old. I can't tell you how grateful I am for these two people who cared for me and my younger brother. I owe them my life and I hope that they know that I will always love them dearly. I just wish that E and L had been more experienced in dealing with a child who had seen some things at a very young age and needed psychological help. Maybe things would've been different for me.

Chapter Two

This lovely couple who already had a house full of children opened their hearts and home to my brother and me. I was two and my brother was nine months old when we were taken in. I'm not sure who was "delivered" first but we ended up together. Dad (L) was a hard-working man. I always noticed growing up that his hands were so rough looking and always had black under his fingernails.

Now, being a full-grown woman, I remember that and it gives me great pride knowing that he worked hard. Those hands were the way they were because of the hard work he did. Dad worked at a printing company. Every night, he would come home and take a tall frozen beer glass out of the freezer. He loved his ice water. He was a dedicated father.

L spent countless hours and sleepless mornings, and a lot of money toting my younger brother to and from hockey. In fact, he did the same for my brother's friend. My brother was always into sports, so we were always going to the games.

I loved when Mom and Dad would take us with them to the racetrack. Dad wasn't the disciplinarian in the house: that was all left to Mom. But let me tell you, if he did get mad, you definitely heard about it. Dad was very active.

When the Earl Grey Swimming Pool was open Dad loved to go swimming. I guess that's why he always stayed fit and energized. He was and is a great father. When the eldest of the kids was doing time in Kingston Penitentiary, we were always driving back-and-forth to Kingston to visit.

If any of his children ever needed him, he was always there… especially financially. I think I am the only one of his kids who has never asked him for money. That's just my character.

All of his friends and coworkers called him "Doc" because he was the weed man back in the day. And now that Mom has passed, I'm beginning to learn more about the man he was, and is, and not just the father figure. I feel blessed that he is showing me that side of him. I love this man dearly and I will forever be grateful to him. I don't believe he has any idea what he means to me. I love you, Dad.

My mom was like me in some sense. Even though we're not blood, now looking back at her through the eyes of a young person and then and as an adult, we have the same characteristics. We both loved to dance, and we both loved to change up our hairstyles. We both wore whatever the hell we wanted to wear and didn't give a crap what anyone thought. We share the same traits of being givers.

But what stands out for me about Mom is the love that she'd receive from everyone who knew her. Our house and our doors were always open. And, oh boy, did she like to smoke her weed. LOL. Mom could throw down in the kitchen too. I loved her meatloaf among many other dishes. She was certainly known for her baked beans (even though I thought they were yucky because I've never been a fan of molasses).

As I sit here and write this in reflection, I have come to the conclusion that Mom needed to be needed. She came from a huge family in the Nova Scotia countryside. I can surmise that, living with so many people, a person can get lost looking for their place in the family.

I don't know, I'm just speculating here but either way, Mom had a heart of gold. There will never be another like her. I miss her every day. I love her dearly and respectfully.

I put both Mom and Dad through hell growing up and, although this is not an excuse, to a certain degree, and in my mind, I felt like I was trapped in hell. Imagine living in your house with the parents who took you in, and then your biological mother, who married your foster/stepbrother, moves in too. And your biological father (Pops) comes and visits Doc from time to time, and leaves you behind, again and again.

I will forever be grateful to these two amazing people I call Mom and Dad. If you are reading this, please know that I love you both deeply.

My mommy, Glenda, was a stunning woman. My firsthand recollection of her is limited, because I was very young when she left me to live with E and Doc, but through the years, I have heard many things that people have said about her. She would come around and take me and my brother on outings—mostly to my nanny's house. But when she married E's eldest son, she moved in with us. It was crazy if you were looking in. I had my Mom, Dad, Mommy, and her husband (foster brother/stepdaddy to me). What I do know with certainty is that she adored me and the feeling was mutual.

The following quotes are just a few of the lovely things that people said about her.

"She was stunningly beautiful."

"When she walked into a room, her very presence commanded attention."

"When she went out to the clubs, people—stunned by her beauty—would stop and stare."

"Both men and women wanted her."

"She was idolized."

There were many more quotes. It seems that only good things were said about Mommy, despite her addiction. The pain and torment placed upon her was never reciprocated. It just wasn't in her heart. If anything, she seemed to treat others far better than she treated herself.

To me, Mommy was a Queen. She was of mixed race: White Irish and Barbadian. She had long legs. She had a caramel complexion, and she had an infectious smile. Many say I have that same smile.

Now, I know many people say, after a person passes away, that they were beautiful, they were this, they were that—but the truth is, she really was a gorgeous woman. Many people tried to take that from her. I wish I could speak more about my mommy from my personal perspective but, as I've said, our time together was limited.

My last time with her will stay with me forever. Certainly until my last breath, I will pay homage to her and my biological Pops, Kirtus. Pops was noticed by women, and many that knew him, said he was fine. Those ocean blue eyes and the space between his teeth sent many a woman swooning for his attention. At least, that's what I was told. Pops was born in Nova Scotia and had many siblings. His mother was my Nanny Flo. Many of Nanny Flo's kids were very tall, at least the males were. Nanny was only four feet something. Yet a powerhouse to be sure.

Pops was a hustler of many things. He was the second youngest of his siblings. He loved music and he loved writing. It's been told that a very famous Canadian musician stole a song Pops had written and it became the musician's number one hit back in the day.

Interesting, isn't it?

I absolutely loved it when Pops would pick me up and take me out to dinner, or shopping. He bought me my first pair of road runner jeans, the album Grease, and he took me for three weeks on a trip to Vancouver. He also took me to Disneyland: A memorable trip that I will cherish forever. I love and miss that man with all of my heart and soul.

I believe Mommy and Pops met in the West End area. Mommy lived in Alexander Park, and I believe Pops went to school nearby. Anyway, they met when they were 15, and they were inseparable.

Some may not believe in true love at that young age; nonetheless, I know my father cared deeply for my mother. Unfortunately that ended when my dad went to jail. I believe he went for about a year, and my mom ended up meeting my brother's father. I've had a few people tell me that dad never forgave my mom and the betrayal broke his heart.

Pops had a lot of girls and women buzzing around and basically, he had his pick of women. But the love between my birth parents was undeniable—they were kinda like Bonnie and Clyde. They were on and off until I was born in 1969. Pops was 19 and Mommy was just turning 19 the same month I was born.

Pops's lady, who I went to spend some time with in Vancouver, told me the same thing. That Pops never forgave her. He was so hurt about Mommy stepping out on him.

One of the greatest gifts Pops gave me was (and still is) my older Sister D. She is one year and one month older than me. We weren't raised together, in fact we met for the first time when I was pregnant with Celeste. That was 28 years ago. This amazing woman I call Sister is a gift from the Creator. D and I are a lot alike but at the same time, complete opposites. I love color, she doesn't. I am loud and at times hard to calm down, where she has a quiet and calm demeanor. And although we are different in many ways, I think it's safe to say, we complete each other. I am very grateful to have her.

Anyway, if you need to know where I got my hustle skills, it's from those two people. So here are my four parents: I have inherited many traits from them. They have each hurt me in some way and I have forgiven them. They have all had a part in shaping the woman I have become.

I love them. How could I not? We have all made mistakes. Lord knows I've made many with my children. So, in order to move forward, I must forgive the past.

Chapter Three

I cannot recall what my biological mother, Glenda—my mommy—told me when I was taken to live with a lady named E. I just knew that she and I were going somewhere. She may have explained to me what was about to take place, but I was too young to remember. What I do recall, however, is watching her leave through the screen door, sobbing my little heart out and begging for her to come back.

All I could comprehend, in my two-year-old mind, is that she brought me to a house with complete strangers and left me there. Today, I wonder what my mommy was feeling when she had to walk away from me after hearing me cry. It's a certainty that she was broken, and I believe that with every ounce of my being. So, it seemed to me that I was abandoned by the love of my life - my mom.

Now that I am older, and I've lived through pretty much everything she has lived through except for leaving this earth, I understand her pain. I know the pain of having children and watching them be raised by somebody other than myself.

I don't remember much that happened after being given up by my mother (which I now know was a selfless act on her part), but I've been told things about my early behavior. My mom relayed to me that I was a very destructive little girl. She said that, when I moved in with her and was allowed to play with my sister's belongings, Apparently, I broke everything that belonged to this sister I suddenly had.

I'm not a psychiatrist, but my mom told me about my destruction of property, and I believe it had everything to do with being left with strangers. Keep in mind, I was two years old when I moved in with them.

As I recall from what was told to me, it makes perfect sense. It's understandable, being as I was abruptly removed from my mother's arms and placed in the care of other people, that I would act out in one way or another. With this in mind, I believe what I was told about this stage of my life.

Here's an interesting story my mom shared with me, about when I first moved in with them. She told me that one evening, she heard a lot of noise coming from the kitchen. She went down to investigate and found two-year-old me in the kitchen, sitting on the floor in front of the wide-open fridge—gorging on a whole cooked chicken.

The theory of this event, from my understanding, was that, while in my biological mother's care, I had to fend for myself and I may have been starving. For all intents and purposes, it was normal for me to find whatever I could and eat it, at any time of the day or night.

Of course, this is pure speculation on my part, but it's logical to me as an adult that it was justifiable behavior. These stories intrigue and upset me all at once. It hurts me, not that I may have had to fend for myself at such a young age, or that there was no food in my mommy's home, but because it is the truth.

Chapter Four

One of my earliest memories was a horrific one. I was three years old. My mom's next-door neighbor was a friend of the family. I guess I would go into his backyard or play in front of the house. I remember him picking me up and sat me on a wooden shelf in his garage, which was in the back of his house, and putting his penis in my mouth.

I don't believe I cried. I didn't say anything to my mom until I was in my late 20s. When I did speak up about what this monster had forced upon my young self, my mom told me that it was just a dream. With every survivor, especially when some time has passed, we begin to question ourselves. We ask ourselves, did this assault really happen? I have questioned myself many times, but I also know what happened to me and this is one hundred percent true.

In regard to the first remembered incident, I received validation from my body's response when I came in contact with him years later. For the purposes of this book, I will call him Joe.

At the age of five, we moved from Langley Street into a house on Blake Street. That was the name of the housing project, and we lived there for twenty-three years. Not far from Blake Street is a Plaza.

I remember my sister, Susie, and I walking through the parking lot from that plaza, and a car drove up. My sister said hello to the guy in the car. It was Joe. As soon as I saw him, my body began to shake uncontrollably. I felt extreme fear. I was terrified and I knew from that moment and for years to come that what I thought happened to me actually did happen.

Chapter Five

The second violation on my body was from a family member when I was the tender age of six years old. It was in the basement of our home. I remember, at that time, we had a pool table and a small couch. My four-year-old brother and I were downstairs, and I don't know if the man was already there, or if he came down after us. I do remember my brother riding his little tricycle around.

This monster laid down on the couch. He was fully clothed, as was I, and he made me lay on top of him. I don't recall touching. I know for sure that there was no penetration because we were fully clothed.

I am still shocked at his boldness because my little brother was right there, but since we were clothed, I guess he thought the act was not visible to my brother. This animal is the family predator and he has touched "accidentally" many children in our family. He has made derogatory comments to my friends. He always looks at them and stares. He kisses his teeth and makes comments and subtle advances.

I've heard many stories of him messing with other family members and about the things that he's done to them. As far as I am concerned, he is a dirty snake. The worst part is that the family knows this. In fact, they've always known what a predatory monster he is, but he was never called out and he was never charged. This doesn't surprise me, given my family's history of addiction and abuse. This family of mine, and I don't say this to be disrespectful, has secrets, skeletons, and demons that most people couldn't even imagine. Everyone in our family is aware of them, but we've always kept them carefully hidden. It's clear to me that this is the reason that my family tree is one steeped in abject alcoholism and drug addiction.

The thing I've learned about my family is that the elders have been victimized in childhood and/or adulthood. Not just the girls and women, but also the boys and men. I found out from my own experience and speculation that nobody wants to talk about abuse. This was definitely the case with my family. We don't want to talk about being sexually assaulted. And? If anyone did, they would most certainly be called out, branded a liar, and would be considered persona non grata. We are made to feel ashamed, and to some degree, we question our own sanity. But as I have mentioned previously, the body has its own memory, and the body does not lie.

The predatory monster I've spoken of in this chapter has never been brought to justice in the legal sense, but I feel by writing accounts of what I was subjected to, I will find my own justice.

Chapter Six

Your home is supposed to be your safe place, right? It's supposed to be the place where you can be free to be yourself without the fear of being hurt. Right? Well, it's not always that way and it wasn't for me.

I was eleven years old and it happened twice. *He* (my abuser) came into my room, a room I shared with my younger brother. I remember it so clearly and, as I sit here remembering, I'm sick to my stomach. Back then, I don't remember ever wearing pajamas that had bottoms. I was wearing one of those long flannel nightgowns when *He* came into our bedroom.

When you entered the bedroom, my brother's bed was on the right side of the wall and my bed was on the left. The physical sensation I am having right now in this memory is just blowing me away. Remember what I mentioned earlier about our bodies and their memories? This is what is happening now. What an awful feeling. Forgive my digression and let me move on.

He came into our room and laid on my bed. *He* raised my nightie, pulled down my panties, and with his underwear down, he began to rub his penis against my vagina. There was no penetration. I don't recall there being any finger touching just his penis. I don't think he ejaculated. I mean really, there would be evidence if he did that. Maybe he did in his underwear or something, I don't know. What I do know is that he did this to me twice. I also look back and wonder how come my younger brother didn't wake up when this was happening. Or was he awake and too afraid to say or do anything? I asked him years later and he said he doesn't remember that.

For years I held this without telling Mom and Dad, but all of my friends knew. My friends knew because I told them right away, but what could they do? I guess I had to tell somebody and I felt safer telling my friend than telling any adults. Was it fear of not being believed? Maybe.

We didn't tell our elders in fear of what would happen to us, and thirty years later, for the exact same reason, we still can't tell. Because when I finally did tell, Mom and Dad didn't validated my concerns. I remember sitting Mom and Dad down in my house and reading them the letter, and Mom categorically denied that this happened to me. She was adamant.

It took me thirty years to share this information and I was crushed even more by her denial. Because of that denial, our relationship had been altered forever. I never went back up to the house until the year before she died. My children and I never went back for dinners or holidays.

But let me give you a little example of my truth. Every morning, before Dad went to work, he always checked in on my younger brother and me. He would check in just to see if we were okay. One morning when he was checking in on us, I jumped up in fear because I thought it was *Him*. And when I looked, it was Dad and he said go back to sleep, and he shut the door. Subconsciously I wasn't going to allow *Him* to do this to me anymore—which is why I kind of jumped up and made a sound hopefully loud enough that someone would hear or *He* would be too afraid that someone heard and run back upstairs. And of course, years later—many, many years later—as I finally spoke my truth again, I was invalidated by everyone in my family. Normally, something like that would have had a very negative effect on a person like myself, sending me right back into the annals of addiction but nope. This was and is the truth although I stood alone, I still stand alone. Sober without validation.

This is part of doing the work on myself and acknowledging and accepting a lot of terrible things that I've done to people and myself. I wanted forgiveness and I am willing to give forgiveness to others. And all I wanted was for *Him* to acknowledge what he had done to me and apologize. I didn't and still wouldn't need the rest of the family to even know that he said those words to me as long as I knew.

You see, I don't care what people think. But he is in his own hell and will continue to be there. I am moving through life stronger because of it.

Chapter Seven

Growing up on Blake Street shaped me, taught me, twisted me, and hurt me. But it still gave me a lot of friendships that I still have today and will always cherish. Of course, we've all grown and have our own families now, but we are still very much a family community. When one of us hurts or falls, we all feel it. When one has passed away, a part of us goes with them.

Like every neighborhood, there are cliques, and our hood was no different. I guess you can say that our cliques randomly changed or maybe it would be better to say that we had cliques within our cliques. And like all preteens and teenagers, we would kick off at times.

Of course, there were physical fights and gossiping but, looking back at it now, it was all just typical teenage crap. What I do remember being hard to deal with in a clique is that, if you were in turmoil or engaging in any kind of argument within the clique, instead of the one person being against you, depending on your place in the hierarchy of popularity, you could end up with your whole clique being against you. That was never a good feeling.

It felt like, to some degree, you were banished. It was a difficult situation because it is human nature for us to want to be liked. I, however, was very resourceful. If I'd been outcast from my group, because of some teenage infraction, I would simply branch out of the community and hang out with other girls I knew from school.

I guess, looking back, those are the incidents that gave me strength or at least an introduction to resilience. Regardless, my Blake Street family was extremely important to me. I guess you can say the hand I was dealt could have been better. Part of me wants to say that I was dealt a hand that was no good, but to say that would mean that everything about my young years was bad and that is just not true.

There was a lot of confusion, that's for sure.

Chapter Eight

I was six years old when my brother became my stepfather. I know that sounds crazy and incestuous, but it really isn't. My brother was not my blood brother; he was the son of my mom, E, and he was much older. I mean, he wasn't a brother—blood or not—and he wasn't a father figure either, for that matter. He just happened to marry my biological mother, Glenda. He was cruel, mean, and violent.

There were always parties growing up at my house, maybe that's where I get the desire to always entertain. I recall one party in particular, in our house on Blake Street. I remember this one clearly because something had happened between my brother/stepdaddy and mother, Glenda. She came upstairs into the bedroom where I was sleeping and laid in bed with me. She wasn't with me for a very long before he burst through the bedroom door demanding her to get downstairs. She didn't want to.

I don't remember the details or the reason she didn't want to go downstairs. Maybe she was tired, I don't know, but he was angry and loud and he didn't seem to care that I was in bed with her. It was as if I was invisible to him.

She said again that she didn't want to go downstairs, and he went to the closet, grabbed a coat hanger, and began striking her with it. My poor mother was screaming, I was crying and, be it the beating, or my crying, she eventually went downstairs. That memory haunts me still. Knowing the life that was placed upon her, the pain and scars and everything that happened to her, it just breaks my heart to this day.

So just know that, as I walk through this gift called life, there has always been a piece of me that has been broken, or better yet, ripped from my body. Is it my place to ask why she married this person? Throughout my adulthood I have been given stories as to why she married someone who was, for all intents and purposes, my brother. I have no opinion either way but, in my heart, I feel sadness for her.

It was all just an extension of the abuse my poor mother had suffered at the hands of the men in her life. She had no concept of a healthy relationship, so she had nothing to compare the broken ones to. It was as if she was subconsciously feeling so unworthy that she felt that she just wanted to continue to hurt. She felt she deserved no better than what she got.

Some may disagree, but in my opinion, nobody marries a monster if they have love for themselves. If you're born into abuse, you just don't know any better, and that is not your fault. My mommy was a victim of circumstance.

On a cold January day in 1981, my mother took her last drug. Somebody intended to kill her and gave her a hot shot, which caused her to take her last breath. She died when I was eleven.

Chapter Nine

Despite all the negativity leading up to my teens, there were a lot of positives growing up as well. I had many friends and we had a blast most times. I went through a lot of experiences with all of them, but there is one who has been with me through almost all of my joys, triumphs, and challenges. My girl, my sister-friend, Corinna. We were the 'bigger' girls of our crew, so the boys of our street gave us not-so-flattering names, which helped mold our low self-esteem and stayed with us throughout our adulthood. Well up until I was smoking crack 24/7. We know you lose weight quick doing that.

The times we had were crazy, scary, and dangerous, but also so much fun. Now you can believe this or not, but I used to be very shy (yes, I know it's hard to believe) growing up. And, well, Corinna taught me some things (laughing out loud). But that's not my training to share. I could write a mini book on her and my friendship and maybe one day I will. Just know she has been my sister-friend since we were small (six or eight) and she has seen me at my worst. For years, we didn't talk because I was in the trenches of my addiction and she couldn't bear to watch me slowly die. And of course, she needed to devote her energy to raising her children. But we found our way back to each other and we haven't left, nor will we. I love you girl.

One fond memory I have is of the donut shop across the street from where I lived. I remember those donuts were so delicious and they were cheap. The only bad thing about that donut shop was that we had to fight the bees to get to our donut. Not to be deterred, we would brave the nasty little stingers and pray that we didn't get stung before we got our sweet treat.

I remember a time when somebody broke into the donut shop. Of course, as youngsters would, we all ran up in that shop snatching up as many donuts as we could. There were donuts all over the place. I recall us having donut fights right in front of the police because, what could they do? I mean I guess they could've prevented us from going in but I think at this point, nobody was in the shop. We had already taken every donut in that damn place and just had a great time.

It was just like a snowball fight but instead of tasteless frozen water, our weapons were sweet, heavenly delights. The police officers just sat in their cars waiting for the owners to come to lock the place back up. They were not interested in harassing us kids.

I was so happy that I was able to steal a huge tray of donuts. Before I even got to the door, however, my mom told me to turn around and take those damn donuts back to the shop. I was embarrassed and so angry. I couldn't understand why my mom made me return them. I mean, really, who turns away free donuts?

We were a fearless bunch. That's the only word I can use to describe us wild teenagers. We would skateboard or roller skate down the Blake Street hill. We would double up on our skateboards. We would sit on them and ride them down the street, hoping that we wouldn't get hit by a car in the process. We were very lucky that we didn't.

In the winter, we would go behind Eastview Community Center with our toboggans and slide down that steep hill. At the bottom of the hill, there were huge rocks bolted by hard wire and we would just fly in the air off of those rocks. The thought of it still makes me smile. The recklessness of our youth would drive us to daring feats.

We would slide our toboggans down the cemetery hill right into the road, hoping again that we wouldn't get hit by a car and, again, feeling lucky that we survived the experience. We would climb up the Geezer hill and onto the rails of the buildings.

I will never forget the times we'd engage in childish pranks like playing the classic game of Nikki Nikki Nine Doors. We tortured the poor people who moved into the houses across the street from us. We would knock on their doors, or ring the bell, and run.

There were a few times I got myself into trouble but, in my exuberant youth, I would not be deterred. One day we were playing a game at 80 Blake Street. I forget the name of the game but what I clearly remember is taking the fire extinguisher out from its enclosure and spraying the contents everywhere. That little stunt earned me a grounding by my mom.

I can't tell you how many times she grounded me. My lust for excitement compelled me to set a school bus on fire. There was a line of cars in front of it and behind it, but I didn't care. The door was open and I set fire to garbage inside the vehicle. Little did I know that, right across the street, my sister was watching. I can't recall if I took a beating for that one, but I was definitely grounded.

I also once again lit a garbage can on fire in the underground parking. Unbeknownst to me, one of the neighbors saw me running from the scene and told my mom. Once again, I was in trouble. Looking back, I realize I could have jeopardized our housing. But in my thirteen-year-old mind, I didn't consider the danger.

Chapter Ten

My mom, for whatever reason, had forbidden me from hanging out at 80 Blake. She must have believed that the building was the source of my misbehavior, because it seemed that most of my shenanigans happened there. Of course her placing a taboo on going there only made it that much more attractive to me. Having to sneak over to 80 Blake fed my need for adventure. Even though sometimes I got caught, nothing ever discouraged me from going over there.

I lost my virginity in that building at a friend's apartment. It happened during a game of Truth, Dare, Double Dare. I don't recall if it was me or the boy who was dared, but the challenge was for us to go into the bedroom. I emerged from that bedroom no longer a virgin.

I remember running into the bathroom. There were maybe ten of us playing the game. I must have looked as terrified as I felt, because everybody was like, "OMG what happened?!" They were patting the boy on the back like he was a hero, but I was scared and embarrassed.

I can't describe the emotional turmoil I was going through at that moment, but I really did like this boy, so part of me was elated that we had been together in the most intimate of ways. The boy, however, was acting like he didn't feel the same way. That being said, it didn't stop him from riding by my house on his bicycle and stopping in front of my house. No words were spoken but I knew exactly what he wanted so I would jump on his bike and go up on the hill behind the building to have sex with him. I was fourteen.

Not long after that, I became pregnant by another boy. a boy who would be forever linked to my heart. The boy that got me pregnant was my boyfriend but we were barely teenagers. I was so afraid to tell my mom that she didn't find out until I was almost four months pregnant.

She eventually found out because Corinna, who was so worried for me, told her mom and her mom called my sister, and so on until it reached my mother E's ears. There was never a question from my mom's perspective about whether I was keeping the baby or not. I was not keeping it and I had no say in the matter. What happened next, being four months into the pregnancy, was a brutal experience. At this point, my then boyfriend became my ex-boyfriend because the pregnancy put such a strain on all of our parents.

It was just a very difficult time for everybody involved. I was forced to have an abortion and I don't recall anybody being there for me. It was a time when I needed my people the most. Aside from mom and my sister, of course, but then who else could really be there for me? We were all teenagers. It was so traumatic because I was so far along in the pregnancy. I had to give birth to the baby but prior to doing that, they had to kill my baby. Just that in itself and having to give birth to a deceased fetus was brutal.

Now, although my mom and sister were there for this procedure, I still felt like I was completely alone. I was truly alone in my young mind with my thoughts, my fears, and my pain. As I mentioned, the father of my would-be child at the time was not around.

I'm not sure if he was forbidden to see me, or he just didn't want to be there for me. Looking back now, what could he do or say? We were kids.

Chapter Eleven

Years after the abortion, maybe twenty or so years ago, I tried to reach out to the would-be father in the hopes of having a conversation with him about what happened. I guess, to some degree, I felt guilty about aborting the pregnancy and I wanted to make amends. I wanted us to talk about it. This was a big loss for me. I don't know how he felt about it.

I could only speculate, but as adults, it would have been nice to be able to talk with him. After all, it wasn't only my child, it was his as well. Who else could I share or express my feelings about it with? Alas, I never got the chance because he chose not to engage in a conversation about it.

I was extremely hurt by his decision but I respected it. Just as I have the right to feel my emotions, so does he. I am grateful because we are still friends today, and I feel no resentment towards him. I guess because it happened to me and my body, I felt, and still feel, more deeply about it than he, and that's fine I have no judgment toward him. That is a loss that I keep deep inside.

I guess I need to go back to when my mother was killed when I was 11 years old, but after my mom's killing and after the abortion, something inside me had changed. I was no longer the same person. However it wasn't all bad.

I remember that same boyfriend wanted to come see me. We were hanging out on the block and I recall him telling me that he was going to come and see me at midnight. I was thinking to myself and asking him, "Are you crazy? How are you going to do that?"

Our house had five bedrooms and I was on the top floor facing the street, so I wondered how he thought he was going to accomplish that at such a late hour. I mean, clearly he wasn't coming through the front door.

What he did was climb on top of a smaller house's roof, then he climbed up onto our roof, and then he climbed into my window. I can't even express how afraid I was for him. Corinna said I was terrified that he would fall. But he didn't. He made it safely into my room through my window.

I don't remember this but Corinna said I was trying to figure out all the different ways to abort the baby myself. I was tobogganing down Riverdale Hill and eating mustard, I don't know. I was desperate and terrified. My fear was not of having the baby. My fear was of, once again, getting in trouble with my mom.

I can't recall if my boyfriend and I broke up after that. What I do know is that we shared something so intimate that no one will ever take it away from us, even if it was for a brief time.

My baby daddies younger sister, Wendy, is one of my dearest most cherished soul sisters. I share that because I want y'all to know how much I love her and appreciate our bond. What took place between her brother and me never affected my friendship with Wendy.

At the tender age of fourteen, in just a matter of months, I lost my virginity to one boy, got pregnant and by another boy, had an abortion and met still another boy who would change my life in ways that I could never imagine.

And not long after that I met another boy who would walk on fire for me.

Chapter Twelve

A new girl had moved to Blake and she asked me and a few of my friends to walk with her to the park – Regent Park, another low-income housing project. She said she had met these guys that moved here from the states. Intrigued, as young girls are at the thought of meeting new boys, we decided to go with her.

Our friend (S) had recently moved into a 3-story building in that particular housing project. When we got there, we were all outside and I remember it so vividly. I was wearing my new baby blue tracksuit. It was the age of breakdancing, and the dancers often wore tracksuits like mine, so I felt like the peak of fashion in that suit. I was rocking my natural S curls with bangs.

The neighborhood boys were outside with us and we had just made introductions. One of the guys called up to Wayne and told him to come on the balcony. They told him that there was a girl down here who he should meet. He came downstairs and asked for my name and number and that was that.

I'm not even sure if it was my phone number he asked for, or if he asked me to go out with him. Either way, I said yes. As my memories fall on that special time, I'm reminded of that special feeling of nervous excitement that seems to be reserved for teenage girls and boys. Believe it or not, I was a very shy person in those days. That was until you got to know me, of course.

I didn't know that the day I left our community to walk all the way down to the Regent Park Community, I would be introduced to this person who would take me on a journey that I couldn't have imagined.

Chapter Thirteen

Can you imagine your fourteen-year-old child being beaten by her sixteen-year-old boyfriend? If one of my daughters was beaten by her boyfriend, I would lose my mind and the boy in question would be, without a doubt, receiving the same pain and more. But it happened to me.

In the span of eight years, Wayne beat me, choked me, raped me, dislocated my hand, stole from me, somehow managed to get glass in my knee … one time he tied me up with a telephone cord and violated me in front of my son. I can't even tell you how many beatings that boy put on me. His brother once stopped him from choking me one second before I passed out. He had me so afraid.

When he stood up, I sat down. When he pretended to come at me, I flinched with total fear. The anxiety is indescribable.

One day, he came to my house with a big stick. I wasn't home but he eventually found me. I remember we were arguing in the back of my sister's house. MM came out and asked me if I was okay. Even though I was far from okay, I said I was. When I was trying to run away from him, "GM" and the other boys also asked me if I was okay.

Wayne said something, and even though I don't remember what he said, it was clearly not nice because Wayne and "GM" began arguing. Wayne was being his aggressive self, and going for "GM", but "GM" put him down in a minute. It was so strange because, as much as I've grown up with all of these guys and they were concerned for me, I actually felt bad for Wayne. In hindsight, I would have to say that this was the beginning of me having the mentality of an abused woman-child

As a fifty-two-year-old woman and a counselor for abused women and children, I can't help asking myself why? Why did I let this happen? Especially at fourteen. For somebody who was looking in from the outside, a more apt question would be, where were my parents or a guardian?

Well, the answer to "why" is that I loved him. He made me laugh. He said he loved me and, at that time in my life, that's what I needed. By the age of fifteen, I was running away from home so I could stay at his house more. His mother allowed her children's boyfriends or girlfriends to sleep over, which of course would never, ever happen in my home. We were allowed to do everything in Wayne's home. Drink, smoke weed, have sex ... pretty much whatever we wanted to do.

Due to the things that had already transpired in my life up to the age, I was very insecure. I was in an emotional black hole. Broken. Lost. When I met Wayne. he filled that emptiness inside—it was an emptiness that my parents, my friends, nor anybody else, had been able to fill.

Now, the answer to the second question: where were my parents? They were home, which was somewhere I didn't want to be. When they found out about him beating me, they tried to intervene, but I was having none of that. I'd lie and say it wasn't happening. I'd tell them right to their faces, "No that's not true."

Chapter Fourteen

Have you ever wished you made different choices in life? Have you ever given up something good for something bad? I have. I guess the real question to ask is, do I regret choosing the bad?

I'll answer that later. But first picture this. I am with my boyfriend, Wayne, riding the Pape bus when our eyes meet. He's staring at me while I'm trying not to let Wayne see me looking back at him. Then it happened again. Another time, on the same bus, I saw him again. He was what you would call a tall, dark, and handsome young man. He was eighteen and I was sixteen. He went to Danforth Tech. He played ball. His name was Tannis.

Now I have always loved to dance. Back in the day, he had a little group called the Oriole Connection. The group consisted of him and two others. He was a good dancer, especially when it came to slow dancing. Wow. I have never slow danced with another man the way I danced with him. When we danced, it was like we became one.

Our number one spot was Club 650—a bar where we used to hang out every weekend. One evening Tannis and I were slow dancing. My cousin slid right up to us and told us to get a room. It looked like we were making love on the dance floor. Not that we were trying to be intentionally sexual, we just moved with such passion. We were so in sync with each other. Any time I hear either of these songs—Between the Sheets by Isley

Brothers or Time Will Reveal by DeBarge—I instantly conjure up memories of Tannis.

Those were our songs. And like I said, no man I've ever danced with in the past or present has moved with me the way he did.

Tannis was so good to me. He was kind, he was generous. When he worked at the Ralph Thornton Center, we would be on the phone for hours and hours. I fell asleep a couple of times on the phone with him. One of us would always say, "You hang up," "No you hang up." LOL.

If you don't know what I'm talking about, this was us as teenagers. When I think of Tannis, I think of unconditional love, real love—just like Mary J's song. Mom and Dad loved him. Mom even allowed him to join us on our family vacation for one year. Now that boy has a story—you'll have to read that one in my next book.

The way he looked at me made me feel nervous. In his eyes, you knew it was nothing but pure love for me. I don't know... I just know that, if at any time of my life—back then right up until today—if I needed anything, this man would help me.

Tannis wanted things for me that I had no idea that I wanted. He encouraged me. He praised me. He had left an imprint on my life and my heart that will stay with me for the rest of my life. He also was the father of my second pregnancy, at age sixteen.

Chapter Fifteen

Tannis and I drifted apart because of, first, being with Wayne and living at his house (although I didn't divulge this info to Tannis until he and I were no longer together). This young man had a goal and had already been working for a couple of years at the Ralph Thornton Center. He went on to a couple of other places of which are elusive to me now. But he had direction. He knew what he wanted, and what he wanted included me.

I can't really say if the pregnancy with Tannis came first or after I made the worst decision of my young life but this awful day that I am about to share with you paved my way into the annals of complete self-hate and destruction. Of course I did not know that then.

It's the afternoon and Wayne and I have just gotten off the Pape bus at Bain Ave. to walk to my house. As we are crossing the street, whom do we see? Tannis is standing there. I think he was either going to or coming from my house looking for me. At this time of my life, I was seeing/going out with both him and Wayne. That day would be the day that I got busted and two people would walk away so hurt by my actions, one being me. Looking back at that day makes me realize that that was the defining moment of my future. My decision that day held my fate.

When Tannis saw me, he immediately asked to speak with me, but I didn't want to because Wayne was with me. I was trying to walk away but he followed me, which pissed off Wayne. Now he and Wayne are having words but simultaneously Tannis is desperately asking me to talk with him. I am panicking, I am embarrassed and afraid. I cannot think straight. I just want to get away from both of them at this point. Somehow, we made it into the 80 Blake building. I am being pulled physically and emotionally in every direction. I am thinking to myself, *I am only 15 years old. Why is this happening to me?*

Believe it or not, this is not the only time I have been in entanglements. On a few other occasions, I have dated more than one person at the same time. Once I was dating three. And yes, every time I got busted. That story will blow your mind; we will save it for another book.

We found ourselves on the first level hallway in the building. Peter Hubba (God rest his soul) was also there, as well as CD. I think Wayne pulled a knife and Hubba stopped him from stabbing Tannis. It was complete insanity and chaotic, and I just wanted this to stop. They both kept asking me to choose between them. I didn't want to, I liked them both. Wayne fed the rebellious part of me, but he also fed the ugliness I felt about myself. He would beat me and tell me he was sorry and that he loved me. Tannis fed the fantasy that I could actually be something and do great things. He praised my writing abilities because I was good at it. He encouraged me to be the best I could be—to stop smoking cigarettes and whatever else I was doing. Wayne was the dark and broken side of me while Tannis was my happy, confident, and hopeful side.

By the end of all the craziness taking place at that moment, Wayne left angry and Tannis followed me home. He kept asking me to choose between them and I did. I chose a life of more pain than I had already experienced in my young life. I painfully and so regrettably chose Wayne. This was the first time a boy/man cried over me. Although it hurt me so bad to see him hurt, it also did something for my sick ego. I regrettably chose Wayne for many reasons yet to unfold but I was not a mean person and it hurt me terribly to hurt Tannis.

Now Tannis's tears manifested a sickness within me that told me that, if a man cried over me ,then he must really love me. And that is what I lived for with all my relationships going forward. I never thought of what proceeded before to cause the tears, I just knew in my sick heart that tears coming from a man's eyes for me was true love. I broke one of the most beautiful soul's heart that day. And unbeknownst to me, I would become a victim umpteen times over—a victim of many circumstances.

I had been messing with Tannis a bit so, of course, I got pregnant. This second pregnancy terrified me because I knew I couldn't have the baby. I had nowhere to bring a baby. I wasn't living at home at the time, I was too busy running the streets. So my choice was to have an abortion. I know this hurt Tannis so badly and it's something that always haunts me, especially since I told him it was a boy.

I knew it was a boy because I saw the baby. I was too far gone in my pregnancy to have a regular DNC and the process of aborting the baby at that point was horrific. They (The OBGYN) first gave me something to insert inside of me and they took a massive needle and put something right into the baby through my pelvic area. I believe the needle was to stop the baby's life and the thing that I had to insert was to bring on the labor.

So I had to go through the process of labor and delivery. It's the same procedure as a full-term pregnancy.

I don't even remember how long I was there, but I remember using the washroom, and a little leg came out of me. I can't even begin to explain the emotional turmoil I went through when I saw this. After that the whole body except for the head was expelled from me. Of course there was panic as I summoned the nurse. She came and helped me get to the bed with this baby hanging out of me from the neck down.

When she got me to the bed she said to me, "When the head comes out, press the button and I'll come back." The baby was already dead, and I couldn't take my eyes off him. His little feet were still together. The same for the baby's hands and of course there was the visual of the baby's penis. When the head finally came out, I didn't call the nurse like I was supposed to do. In fact I laid with this baby for a good half hour or more just staring at him. I can't even describe the color of this baby, but it was a pinkish cream color. I was so sad.

I felt empty and confused. How could I have done this? I'd already suffered the plight of being forced to have an abortion, so why would I do this again? I don't think I've ever felt so lonely as I did when I was lying in bed with my deceased baby. But I did it and I had to live with that and so did Tannis.

He did try one more time to "rescue" me from the dark and nasty streets of Regent Park but I was having none of it. Years later he told me about the time he was going to Barbados. He admitted that he had even thought of kidnapping me and taking me on the plane with him. At a point when my addiction felt like my worst enemy, I wished he had kidnapped me. He also told me that, when he got married, if I had walked through those chapel doors during the ceremony, he would not have said, "I do." Instead he would have left his bride at the altar to be with me. I was his first love, after all, and you never forget your first love. I was his first sexual experience. Tannis will always have a place in my heart. We are still friends today and will always be, until either of us take our last breath. I didn't tell Mom or Dad what had happened but they found out when a bill from the hospital landed at my parents' feet.

Mom lost it. She went off on me asking me if I wanted to die. I was so upset and embarrassed because the house was full of people at the time. What a terrible feeling. I believe that this was the real tragic end to my relationship with Tannis.

Chapter Sixteen

For the next couple of years I continued to run the streets. Again, I found myself pregnant.

This time, I had my son. But I was still using drugs and drinking. I remember being eight months pregnant and falling down a flight of stairs. When I landed at the bottom, all I could do was laugh.

I was marginally homeless at the time and stuck in a reality that is now known as couch-surfing.

Once again, I asked Mom and Dad if I could come home and, once again, they welcomed me. I was especially grateful since I was mere months from giving birth.

Mom and Dad had no idea of my increasingly dire drug use. I was still using but clearly not the way I was when I was on the streets of Regent Park. But addiction has a funny way of holding onto you even though you may think you have let go of it.

Six months after giving birth to my son, Cameron, I got a call from Community Housing: They gave me an apartment in Regent Park. Looking back now, I like to wonder if I didn't accept that place, would I still have gone down further in my addiction?

But of course, with what I know about the disease now, it wouldn't have mattered where I moved. I could've moved to Timbuktu, it wouldn't have mattered. My addiction always came with me. So now, I was in Regent Park with my son and a dangerous crack addiction, and nobody to stop me from using.

The Insanity of Active Addiction

Incidents of Insanity - Intro

There are so many insane episodes because of my mental enslavement to crack. In fact, I could probably fill three more books with them. But that is not the purpose for me writing this book. I couldn't possibly put these incidents into chronological order because, even though I can recall them with crystal clarity, I couldn't tell you when they happened or even the order in which they happened. At this part of my life, I had no concept of time or how long a day even lasted. There was a point in my active addiction when I ran on crack for ten days without rest. Can you imagine how riddled with insanity a person gets after ten days with no sleep? There was probably no food or water either. I mean, was I even getting high? Probably not. I was simply chasing that first euphoric hit of crack.

And let me tell you something you may not know. The first high is so elusive that it can never be recaptured. Believe me, I spent years chasing it. But I digress, let me tell you some of the wild antics I got up to.

Being a Woman Addicted to Crack

If I thought my life was a mess and completely out of control before that first hit of crack, I found out very quickly how much

45

further down I could slide. The decline was fast and steep. And at the bottom, I got stuck.

Those early days were like a dream. I literally felt like I was in a trance—especially since, in the beginning, I wasn't drinking and using at the same time. When I drank alcohol, it made me feel less "stuck." I figured out that, if I drank alcohol, it would lessen the effects of being paranoid or sounding like I had marbles in my mouth. It definitely alleviated that yucky "stuck" feeling. I figured it balanced out the high.

However, I didn't know about that in the beginning. It's not like there is a manual on how to smoke crack cocaine without becoming a paranoid lunatic. Everyone's using and side effects of using are different. I have seen some crazy shit happen while people were using. One guy I knew back in the day would strip naked and climb a tree. People would have to wait for his high to mellow out before he would come down. Another person, when he smoked dope, would not allow anyone in the same room as him to leave. He would be pacing back and forth with a butcher knife. Crazy times and this was my life. It's kind of funny to think about it now. Using was my sole job in life and mastering it to my level of entertainment took years of practice, thousands and thousands of dollars, and many unhappy people.

I didn't have much money before entering this new level of hell. Now that I had found this drug that I loved and hated at the same time, it was even harder on my almost empty pockets. Sitting in a room with other smokers hoping somebody would give me a hit was my first go-to.

But damned, I could be sitting there for hours before someone gave me a little crumb. It was humiliating, I was begging with my eyes just like the family dog at the dinner table. Sometimes I would come right out and ask.

There were smokers who dealt a little here and there to cover their addiction, and there were dealers. These folks, of course, wanted sexual – favors. Now let me state this right now before I go forward with this entry: In this game of hustling, anyone who traded anything for sex is a trick. The bag holders would always challenge that fact, but I'm here to tell you straight. I don't care if you have money or dope or anything desired by an addicted person: If you trade what you have for sexual gratification, you are a trick. PERIOD!!!

Whomever was holding the bag would want sexual deeds done in exchange for dope. In other words, they were all "tricks." It was disgusting and humiliating and just plain dirty. The dealers knew they had the power. There were many times where I would perform a sexual act and not even get the drugs after. Even now it's hard to describe the defeat and degradation I felt. That feeling only added to the insanity that was manifested deep inside of me.

It's different when you're turning a 'regular' trick because you know what to expect. Most times there are no issues and the transaction would be as it should be. So performing for a bag holder is a whole different danger because these fuckers are high, unpredictable, grimy, and not trustworthy. As I'm writing this, I'm chuckling to myself because, in that world, it's an entirely grimy game. Whether it's for a bag holder or for cold hard cash, it's always grimy and dangerous.

I'd entered this new world that required me to transform into a different person: A person with no self-respect, no concern for others, no moral compass, and no feelings. Admittedly, having no feelings was, in some twisted way, a blessing: Holding yourself and others in such low esteem makes it easier to endure when your feelings are numb. I lied, coerced, threatened, manipulated, and when none of that worked, I carried out the threats and resorted to violence. The hard truth is this: a woman who is addicted to crack is living a nightmare and, a self-degrading existence.

Turning Tricks

I can recall the day I turned my first trick as if it was yesterday. It began with me and another girl getting high together. Of course we eventually ran out of dope. In our jonesing state, our minds naturally turned to scheming and figuring out how to get money for more crack. It was a familiar process. The getting, using, and finding ways to get more. Then the girl suggested something to me that I would not have thought of myself, and even though I can't remember her name, I don't think I'll ever forget the proposition she made.

She suggested that I could make some money in the sex trade. She walked me over to a popular "stroll" and gave me a few safety tips. Looking back, I suspect my safety was not at the forefront of her mind, nor was it at the forefront of mine, for that matter. I'm sure you can guess that the only thing on either of our minds was crack. The memory of how that first trick made me feel is lucid, even after all these years. I was sick with disgust. It was a nasty feeling that could only be quelled with the euphoria of the crack.

There was gold out on the street and it took zero time for me to swallow my pride, what little I had, anyway. Of course gold is a euphemism for the cheap, low paying tricks. They knew they could low ball us because of our addiction, and they did. But any amount of money is gold when you are jonesing. I had crossed a line and entered the world of low track prostitution and the crack pipe was my insatiable pimp.

My Home & Crackhouse

Now that I was granted housing, I felt like I was finally free to do what I wanted. I could smoke crack to my heart's desire without sneaking around. I didn't have to deal with the unique paranoia that comes with trying to act straight around my people. When Mom came around to my place to see the baby, I would hide the crack pipes behind the stove. She was blissfully unaware.

It wasn't long before I was letting people use my apartment for various indiscretions, whether it was letting homeless people use needles in my bathroom, or letting hookers in to turn tricks. People would come over, looking for a safe place to smoke crack, away from the constant presence of the cops who roamed the "crack-hood."

Of course, nobody entered my apartment for free. It would cost them a portion of their dope. The longer they stayed, the more dope I demanded. I would get what is known as "house tokes" and, on some occasions, I would get cash.

It was a cold and dismal existence, but in my crackhead mind, I had hit pay dirt. I also had a safe place to apply my trade and would frequently bring tricks to my apartment. Another thing that was a normal sight in my apartment was the crack dealers. I would allow them to set up in my place and sell crack.

This was probably the most lucrative deal for me because the dealer would pay me to sell in my place. Also, each time someone would come to buy, they wouldn't be leaving my apartment without giving me a toke. So I was basically double-dipping. My son was exposed to this wicked way of life and forced to experience the constant stream of hookers, dealers, and tricks. Frequently my baby was jolted out of sleep by screaming and fighting.

Through all of this, I got pregnant with my daughter, which is certain proof that this type of addiction is so strong, it makes you not care about anything else. Crack was my pimp, my lover, my best friend, and my reason for getting out of bed. The sad truth was this: Nothing came close to being more important than this truly demonic drug. I would have given up every basic human need if it got in the way of my crack use. One thing that got in the way of my crack use was rent. It was cutting into my dope budget and, eventually, I was evicted for non-payment of rent.

A Pivotal Point

After I'd been evicted from housing, I had to move home to my mom's house with my son. As I mentioned, I was very pregnant at the time. Mere days after giving birth to my daughter, my mom received devastating news: Her son, who had been living in Vancouver, had been killed. So on top of having me and my small children to deal with, she had to make arrangements for her deceased son. It was a brutal time for my family.

One day, my mom sent me to buy diapers for the baby, so my son and I set off to the store. Did we make it to the store? No, because money in my hand translated into crack in my pipe.

I went to a friend's house, with my little boy in tow, and started to smoke crack. While I was at my friend's place, for some insane reason, I, high as a kite, decided to give my little boy a haircut. Being as wasted as I was, of course, I did an atrocious job. I mean, seriously, I could have easily cut off one of his little ears.

It didn't take long before I was jonesing. By now, I'd been gone from my mom's house for a long time—way beyond the time it would have taken to buy diapers. And of course I didn't have them. So I guess I told myself that I could turn a quick trick and replenish the diaper money. But deep down, I knew that it was the crack pipe (aka my pimp) lying to me. I would not be replenishing anything but the sweet high of crack. After I'd finished with the trick, I was in a jonesing state, and dying to get high.

Now, I couldn't possibly take the time, or the effort, to drop my son off at my mom's house—especially, since I'd been gone for hours, and I would not be returning with diapers. I did the unthinkable. I sent my son off with a trick—a complete stranger—to my mom's house. Anything could have happened to my boy, but it all made perfect sense in my crack addicted mind. Now, can you imagine the horror that this poor woman felt when a stranger showed up at her door with her grandson? And with a frightful haircut! I couldn't even begin to imagine what went through her mind right then.

I can tell you this for sure: If one of my kids put their child in that kind of danger, I would take that baby, and I would never let my kid within inches of my grandchild. But that was then. By this time, I was past the point of no return and on a mad run. My poor baby boy had become a burden to me. He was simply in the way.

I was too ashamed to face my mom and, fueled by crack, I continued on with my insane dope run. My mom sent people out to find me and nobody could because I was hiding in the darkest places. Figuratively and literally.

As I said earlier, my mother had just found out that her son had been killed. But I was so out of my head and alternating between the short euphoric high and jonesing for crack that I didn't care. In fact, I didn't give a sweet shit about anybody or anything. Except, of course, the crack pipe. After an exhaustive and fruitless search for me, and barely having the strength to deal with her own tragedy, my mom ended up calling Children's Aid and my babies were placed into foster care.

I went to family court and was told if I could stay off the drugs for six months, I would be able to take my children home.

I didn't even really try to stop. I was homeless and my heartbeats had been taken from me. I had no hope, and strong desire to use to numb the pain of that deep loss.

Being the brilliant crackhead that I thought I was, I came up with a genius plan. I would blame everyone but myself for my life being the way it was. This allowed me to condone my deathly behavior. But don't get me wrong, I ached for my kids. Just not enough to stop.

How brilliant was I? Sick right? I went to court for the first six months and the crown extended my help for another six months. Of course I fucked it up and, months later, the courts gave custody to Mom and Dad. Back then, when it happened, I hated them for taking my kids. But of course later, I became so grateful. I don't know what Mom was thinking, I guess in her heart, she held out hope that I would stop using and become the mother my babies needed and deserved.

This was one of several pivotal events, because now, my people were acutely aware of how dark and deep my addiction really was. I was full of shame, but that didn't stop me from using. I actually used those feelings of guilt and shame as an excuse to carry on with my constant crack run.

Another Pivotal Point

One day, I was sitting on a bench on River Street, jonesing and hoping a trick would come by so I could score some crack. This man was walking by with a case of beer. At this point, anything to relieve my cravings would do. So I called out to him and asked if I could have one of his beers.

This handsome man invited me up to have some beers and , of course, I followed. His name was Kwasi. I went to his apartment, and basically, I never left. He fell in love with me, even though my love was crack. I fell in love with what he could provide to me at that time. He had a roof over his head, food in his fridge, and some money in his pocket. I didn't know this man from Adam but here I was, about to destroy another person's life.

I think I was craving some sort of normalcy and I fell in love with the idea of being part of somebody. He became my husband and the father of my three youngest children. Being with Kwasi gave me that stability. I'd like to say that this was the point where I put down the crack pipe, but alas, that was not the case.

Instead of Kwasi turning me from a crack hoe to a wife and mother, I turned him from an actor to a crack dealer and, of course, a trick to other girls who were smokers. I do not label him to be disrespectful. I say it because that is my opinion and perception of him and his movements at that time.

I put him through a lot of shit, I can tell you that for sure. Our time together was a regular series of slow burns that led up to an explosive crescendo. After the climactic blow up, the slow burn would begin once again. This, what can only be described as a rollercoaster of a relationship, was a direct result of my active addiction. It began as a means to an end, and it was a volatile relationship throughout.

The truth is, Kwasi enabled my drug use. He tried to get me to use moderately but, as you will see in later chapters, I could not, or simply would not, comply. That poor man. I put him through hell. He was tortured by me physically, emotionally, mentally, and financially. To this day, I regret all of what I put him through.

Kwasi and I spent 12 years together, all of which were while I was in active addiction. During my many "wanting more crack" insane episodes, I sliced his throat, I burned his chest with a hot iron, I chopped a piece of his ear off. He found me in our bed with another man. I busted his head open with beer bottles and cans, I ripped out 80% of his dreadlocks when he had them, and he had to cut off what was left of them. While in my fits of rage, I would do anything I needed to do to get what I wanted and, if nothing worked, I acted out in revenge. My madness was real. The assaults on this man from my hands and my crazy mind only stopped when I got what I wanted. How he forgave me, I'll never know. Well I do know, and it hurts me to know how I have hurt him. But again, that was my very sick demonized mind and spirit at that time.

The Balcony Incident

In the dangerous game I was playing, there was a lot of deceit, and I had learned, through coercion, manipulation, and threats, how to play the game. What's more, I'm here to tell you that my using, and basically my life depended on how well I played that game. The details of this particular incident elude me today, but I remember clearly the key point of it.

Kwasi's apartment was on the fourteenth floor of a high rise. It was my main home but, as I said, I would give my body and soul to anybody who I could get money or dope out of.

At the time, I was semi-living with Kwasi and I pretty much turned his house into a place to smoke crack, but I was also "dating" Charles at the time. I think I must've robbed him or done something to bring him to a state of rage. Whatever the reason, it ended with Charles busting through Kwasi's door. He clearly was furious with me, and my instinct was to escape. I ran to the fourteenth-floor balcony and I literally climbed over the railing, and was hanging there. I guess I would rather have died than deal with whatever situation was happening at the time. Charles couldn't believe his eyes and was so freaked out, he ran out of that apartment. His rage had now turned to fear and disbelief. He was so shocked that I had climbed over the railing. Naturally, he wanted no part of an investigation into me plunging to my death.

Crackhouse Labor

So I was pregnant with my daughter and continued to smoke crack throughout the pregnancy, The baby growing inside of me had no influence over my addiction. Close to term, I was in a crack house, smoking of course, and I started feeling pains. Even in my cracked riddled head, I monitored the contractions, and prayed that they would stop, but they didn't. The dope clearly wasn't helping with the pain so, after an hour of stalling, I walked alone from the Regent Park crackhouse, to St Michael's Hospital.

It was an awful experience to say the least. I couldn't get an epidural or anything for the pain because she was so close to arriving. Within about thirty minutes, I gave birth to my daughter. She was the smallest of all of my children. I think she was like five pounds and six ounces. I'm not a hundred percent sure, but she was certainly in that weight range. She had to live in an incubator for a little while because she had some fluid in her lungs.

As it turns out, I had a sexually transmitted disease called chlamydia at that time and I didn't know it. Giving birth to her vaginally was dangerous because she could've gone blind if the infection had gotten in her eyes. This was explained to me, as if it was the only thing that could've happened to her throughout the time she lived in my belly. Of course, the story around the family throughout her whole life was that she was a drug-addicted baby. But that rumor was clearly bullshit. If this child had been addicted to drugs when I gave birth to her, Child Protective Services would have swooped in and removed her from my care. I was able to leave with her from the hospital, so obviously they saw no danger. Unfortunately, people continued to feed lies to my daughter as she grew into an adult. You will see in later chapters the damage those rumors did to our relationship.

Crack and Motherhood

There is a lot of shame attached to my crack-induced shenanigans, but the memories that haunt me the most, are the ones that involve my children. For instance, there was the time that I was on a run and hadn't been home in three or four days. I was out gallivanting, smoking crack, and drinking nonstop in Regent Park. I had just given birth to Cheyenne. She was maybe a month old at the time. I remember coming home finally and, of course, Kwasi was so angry with me, but he had also been terrified that I may be dead in the gutter somewhere, because I would never answer my phone.

Kwasi was clueless when it came to bathing babies, especially in the kitchen sink that doubled as a baby bath (all the babies were bathed that way in my family).

When I came home, I was still completely wired. The plain truth is, the only reason I came home was because I had no more money and I was fresh out of hustle. The only choice left for me was to go home. When I arrived, Kwasi immediately told me the baby needed a bath.

Now at this point I was still vibrating from all of the drugs I'd consumed over the past seventy-two hours. I wanted to get the task over with ASAP so I was rushing and crashing hard from the comedown. Remember I had been up for three days so I was exhausted as well. I am exhausted. All I wanted to do at this point was go to bed.

Instead of putting the stopper in the sink and filling it with water, which I would have ordinarily done, I just sat the baby in it and ran the water. I began washing my child but somehow, in the process, her toe got caught in the sink drain. When I tried to lift her out of the sink, she was stuck. So, of course, now I am in panic mode. I didn't need Kwasi to see this so, not unlike ripping off a Band-Aid, I yanked her to dislodge her toe. The poor thing was crying and her toe was bleeding.

I don't remember if Kwasi found out at the time, I can only recall the panic and fear I felt within me. I remember thinking, number one: I didn't want to get caught, number two: my baby was hurt, and number three: I must be the worst person in the world. Today, Cheyenne is twenty-five and she still has the scar on her toe. She never knew what it was from until I told her as I was writing this book.

One day I was smoking dope and drinking, and it was actually one of those rare good days—the sun was shining and I was feeling great. My young daughter, Cheyenne, had put some kind of candy in her mouth and she was running through the house. All of a sudden, the candy got stuck in her throat. She came running to me holding her neck and gasping for air. I could see that she was choking.

As you can imagine, I was freaking out as my little girl was trying to breathe. I'd heard somewhere that if someone is choking, they are supposed to raise their arms over their head. I had no idea what to do except tell her to do just that. I was just about to call 911 when the candy dissolved in her throat. I was terrified for her, and also for myself.

To be honest, though, my thoughts were on my high. I didn't want a visit from the paramedics, and possibly the police, interfering with it. You see all of these things that I have shared only a fraction of what I've experienced or force others to experience is what drugs do to you. Addiction enslaves you, and since you can only serve one master, crack was mine.

Death Wishing

Another incident that happened was of the time I didn't want to live anymore. I had no money and, of course, no drugs. I called my girlfriend "CD" who I probably hadn't spoken to in quite some time because of my drug use. There were a couple of reasons that I reached out to her. Those reasons were not what I'd call honorable.

I called her because I was broke and I needed to get high because I was crashing hard. Also I hadn't paid my rent. I remember telling her that I wanted to jump off my balcony. I was living at Main Square at this time, so as I proceeded to tell her this and feeling it with all of my being. This girl told me to do it. She said, and I quote, "Go ahead and jump. You're only going to bounce back up because God doesn't want you."

At first, I was shocked but once her words really sank in, I could not help laughing. In utter and complete despair, yet, in that moment, all I could do was laugh. I'll always remember that, and the memory always makes me laugh.

The Temper Tantrum

Another incident was the day that I went to Kwasi's home, where my children also lived. At this point, I had been forced out of my home by Native Child and family services. I was still using.

Once again, homeless and separated from my children by this crippling addiction. My insane thought process was justifying it all because my husband was selling it. So I went to the house because I knew Kwasi was holding.

I don't remember the children being present because my one-track mind was focused on crack. I wanted the dope yet my husband refused to give me any. I remember sitting on the floor with my legs crossed and having an absolute temper tantrum, not unlike a two-year-old who wants more candy. Have you ever seen a child threaten to stop breathing if they didn't get their way? Similarly, I refused to move unless I got my way. I wasn't going anywhere until he gave in.

Thinking back, I figure the children had to have been there and witnessed the whole shameless act, because Kwasi gave in and I got what I came for. It didn't matter to me that the children were there. I had to have that nasty dope at any cost and the cost was higher than any amount of money. If the kids weren't there, I probably wouldn't have got what I wanted. After he gave me the dope, I left without a backwards glance and went about my business.

Throughout my years of active addiction I have been raped many times. I recall one time being sodomized with a broom stick. Another time being forced into a garbage shoot and raped. I would be picked up by one guy only to enter a home with six more guys waiting for me. You can only imagine what happened there.

I always felt like these assaults were my own doing. I thought that if I wasn't using or solicitating myself, these things wouldn't have happened to me. I know today that I was wrong. Being a drug addict doesn't give others free access to my body when I say "no." Being a sex worker doesn't give someone free reign to my body without my consent. I know a lot of ignorant people will disagree and that's their choice. But NO MEANS NO, whatever my lifestyle is.

The incidents, episodes, and madness from my using years are many. I was dragged from a moving car. I was made to strip down naked by police at 51 Division, outside at Parliament and Dundas when they had a gas station there. I was locked in an elevator with two officers choking me to give up the dope that was in my mouth only for me to thankfully swallow it even with their hands around my neck. I was with a dealer at a house on Dundas only to get raided five minutes after we got there. The guy swallowed all of his bag of dope only to die from it a few hours later.

I saved a girl from dying while we were all smoking. She was a greedy smoker and wouldn't take a moment to enjoy the high, and because of that she did what is called "the chicken"-. She overdosed. That was so scary. I witnessed something like that before.

I have seen guns drawn on people in front of me and I wasn't shaken. The things that I have done to people were treacherous. The things that were done to me were treacherous. The whole dark drug world is one you don't want to play with. Many won't see daylight again and some simply don't survive.

An Almost Fatal Lie

John was sleeping at the table with his crack pipe full of residue. At this time, I was living in Regent with my eldest child, and to be honest, I don't even know where he was at the time. He was only a baby. Wayne's mother Dee and I managed to get our hands on the crack pipe and we cleaned it, smoked it. and then put it back. John didn't wake up and now we were high and jonesing. I wanted more so we cleaned that pipe probably five or six times until it was clean as a whistle.

Well, when John woke up and saw that we cleaned his pipe, he went off. Now this person was known to everybody as a knife wielding bandit. He would slice you with a quickness and not even blink.

Knowing that this crazy man would slice us without another thought, we lied and told him that Dee's son did it. Of course John left the house in a rage because his "wake-up" had been stolen. Freaking out, he left the apartment in search of Dee's son. In our drug fueled state, we didn't realize that we had pretty much signed off on Dee's son getting badly hurt. When he returned, his face was sliced from the top of his cheekbone down to his mouth. His face was wide open and it was because of us.

Talk about being terrified. Of course the police came, and Dee's son went to the hospital. The police charged John with attempted murder. But there had been another incident when John went to jail, and John's people got a hold of Dee's son and beat him so badly that he refused to go to court this time to testify. All of this because his mother and I lied about cleaning John's pipe and smoking the resin.

2
An Extreme & Violent Climax

I've always heard people say that they don't regret anything they've done because the things that they've done or experienced is what made them who they are today. I agree with that statement to a point.

Many of the experiences I've had have molded me and given me the understanding, the empathy, the compassion to be the counselor that I am. It has blessed me with love for others but, also, I have the gift of passion and drive to help others escape things that have boxed them in and kept them stuck.

On the flipside of that, there are many, many things that I wish I never had done. Thinking of those ones makes me physically sick. Because of those ones, I'll will always be making " living amends."

One such incident happened when I was living at Victoria Park and Lawrence with Mary.

I had just left the home of my friend, Trish. Mary was another person that I, in all honestly, took advantage of. I liked her, I liked her home. The best part about her was that she was a crack addict. I hate to say it but, at that time, it was perfect.

By now, my oldest son was acting up. My mom and dad could no longer deal with him, so they dropped him off at my doorstep and drove off. He was a teenager and full of anger and resentment toward me and the life I'd chosen.

He had already been in and out of jail. He was rebellious and doing what he wanted, which was smoking, drinking, stealing, and other crimes.

He was introduced to a crack dealer I used and he immediately became his "soldier." It was a win-win for everybody. Cameron had not always been around me but, unfortunately, he knew more about my business because of the dealer, at least to some degree. In my son, the dealer found a sidekick that could run with him at all hours of the night. My son became a protege to guide through the lifestyle.

I mean really, the dealer wasn't all bad. It's strange because that dealer and I were kicking it and it was always good until I acted out with my temper tantrums to get dope. One evening, a bunch of us were in the apartment and I had already been up for three days. No sleep and living on a steady diet of alcohol, pills, and crack. Ironically, I was to attend the Renascent Treatment facility for the second time a few days later.

Well, I had no more drugs and as usual, the jonesing took over. I wanted some drugs and I think I asked my son for some because, by now, he was actually dealing. Of course he said no.

It wasn't just the answer that set me off, it was the disrespectful way he told me no. He began calling me names, one of which was the disgusting name that we all hated to be called: crack whore.

Looking at it now, through a different lens today, I understand the emotions he was feeling. The embarrassment of his mother bringing tricks into the apartment and taking them straight to the bedroom. Or when a bunch of us were going to the back room to smoke crack.

I wouldn't allow him in the room because I didn't want him to see me that way. This, of course, forced him into isolation. Knowing that he wasn't raised by me for that reason—now he's older and witnessing it with his own eyes.

I get it, I really do. However, at that time and where I was mentally, emotionally and physically, it was a recipe for a disastrous climax. I was a ticking time bomb and I exploded. As soon as he said those words to me, I picked up a butcher knife. I was enraged. I was embarrassed. I was jonesing. Those words cut me like a knife. How dare he say those words to me, especially in front of people.

I threw the knife and it stuck him in his back. Of course I didn't want to kill my child. But in my rage, I became something else. It happened within a split second. I was already regretting it as the knife left my hand, but at that point, I was incapable of stopping. Blood was coming fast from my child.

Of course, everybody in the house was in panic mode and screaming and running out because they couldn't believe what I had done. I was freaking out because I didn't want the police to come, nor did I want him to go to the hospital. Of course I tried to tend to him, to see how bad the wound was. It was mayhem. Nobody could comprehend that I had done this to my own child. The dealer was screaming at me and calling me names.

He was running towards me, but before he could get to me, I picked up one of those ashtrays that weighed like five pounds and, just as I was ready to smash him in his face with it, he stopped because he knew I wasn't playing. At this point, I'm like a dog who is backed into a corner. I was in defensive mode, and my instinct was to protect myself. In tandem, I'm feeling the need to check on my son. I was concerned, too, that I was going to end up in jail.

Through all of those thoughts running through my mind, the dominant thought was, "how could I parlay this incident into getting a hit of crack?" I mean, if I was jonesing before, believe me, my craving for a hit was now tenfold. Soon the desire for a hit of crack was my only thought. It was fortunate at the time that my son did not want to go to the hospital. I can't tell you if my switch to motherhood was born of instinct to save my son or another ploy to get more crack. That's how strong the demon drug had a hold of me. I was a slave to it.

Either way, I stepped in to stop the flow of blood, all the time telling my son how sorry I was. At the same time, I was wondering how I could get some dope. In the calm after the storm, I somehow managed to get more dope and continued to use until I went to treatment.

Of all of the insane things live experienced these ones below hurt my soul deeply.

Who ties up a person with a telephone cord and rapes them in front of their child? It was done to me.

Who threatens to set someone on fire until they surrender their jewels so they can be pawned for dope? I did.

I have woken up to a man inside of me, paid by a dealer to a family member, while I was passed out drunk.

A guy I was dating told me he fucked me while I slept. Before he told me this, I half-asleep realized I no longer had my tampon in. I was puzzled, afraid, and disgusted. What kind of person does this? He was an established businessman.

He rarely drank and did no drugs. But trust me when I tell you, you don't really know people. They only show you what they want you to see.

My mental state of mind was deranged. I would sit with myself and plot what I was going to do to people who had wronged me, and those thoughts were deadly ... or could and would have been ... if I had followed through.

There are so many other stories and drug and criminal ugliness I can share with you but I think you get the gist of what I am trying to share. Horrifying violations were done to me and I did some awful shit to others as well. Take it from me, I still carry all of those scars, most of which are internal. And I am very much haunted by them all. Those memories show up in forms of panic, anxiety, and disassociation. I just try to remind myself that they are just that, they are memories.

Recovery: Trial : Error Acceptance

Chapter One

My first stab at gaining control over my using, and my need to stop letting others down (especially Kwasi), came with me vowing to give up the crack for good. But wait, that was not really what happened. The truth is I was coerced into stopping and I did. At least, until I had money or another "score" of some kind. The lines get really blurry here.

I still wanted to use but I didn't want to spend all my rent money, or sell my jewelry, or sell my TV. I would put empty envelopes in the bank machines to withdraw from the kids' bank accounts, borrow money, turn tricks, or steal from my husband.

That poor man. I robbed him for probably a quarter of a million dollars during our twelve years together. But like I said, despite all of that, along with not sleeping for up to ten days, barely eating, becoming dangerously violent, jumping in and out of psychosis, scamming and scheming, I still wanted to use.

But I was done, or should I say, before the street drugs, pills and booze were done with me. So what do you do when even the drugs don't want *you* anymore? Or you wake up every day despite not wanting to, hoping the Creator would let you die in your sleep? The answer is simple but the process is not. You get clean or die trying.

Chapter Two

My trying to control my using, began with me promising Kwasi I would only drink beer and stay away from hard liquor. As I am writing this, I'm thinking back to the delusional head space I was in trying this method. But hey, I still got to drink, right? We both thought this would stop the crack from entering my mind. But no, crack was on my mind every waking moment and in most of my dreams (whether I was awake or sleeping) too.

When that didn't work, I remember signing a make-shift contract with him promising to stop the using at midnight, and even had a friend at the time witness it. Well, twelve midnight came and went with us fighting because I wanted to continue using. Which I did for the next two days.

There is simply no reasoning with a person in active addiction. These scenarios went on for years.

One time he and I both ended up in jail. Many other times, the police were called because I would get loud and violent, and I wanted him removed so I could keep getting high.

Finally I was beaten down enough that treatment was my only option. I found a counselor. I spoke with her for a while about nothing really. I told her I was there because my husband wanted me to stop using drugs. I wanted to be there, and I didn't want to be there. I really wanted to learn how to use safely. I didn't want to stop. So when she suggested harm reduction and explained to me what that was. I was so happy.! Now I could go back to him and tell him that the counselor said that I could still use, but I could somehow control it. Of course he wasn't going for that, but I stressed to him that this was direction from a professional person, so she knew what she was talking about.

Let's just say that gave me a little bit more time to use but it always ended up the same. Ugly.

I went to treatment.

I walked in dirty and came out clean. I think the worst part of being there was that I had to celebrate Christmas and New Year's there. Not being with my children at that time was the first time I've ever been away from them.

Chapter Three

Life chose me and gave me a second chance at it. It was certainly a gift and a blessing. As much as I wanted it, I didn't want to do the work to receive it ...... until...

There are many "untils" as you've read in the previous chapters. There are actually more "untils" than I can remember so not all of those "untils" have been documented in this book. You would think not being able to remember would give me good reason to stop killing myself. I wanted it but not enough to muster up the motivation or the courage.

My mental obsession for crack had weakened me and I just couldn't wholly commit my mind, body, and spirit to long-term sobriety. There is much more to recovery than simply quitting the drugs. Not using was actually the easiest part. Because the obsession for crack itself lived in my brain, there was a constant battle between doing the next right thing and giving in to the drugs.

Sobriety did not come easy for me, and I don't believe it comes easy for anybody.

My personal journey has been one with many winding roads.

I have been in treatment three times. The first time, I opted for an outpatient program. But I clearly needed more than an outpatient program could offer me. Not only was I *not* a hundred percent in, which I feel is necessary when left to your own devices at the end of the day, but the triggers and easy access to dope, were very hard to deal with.

The following two treatment programs were residential. But let's face it, though, even when you have twenty-four-hour staffing and structured programming, if you are not a hundred percent in, you are doomed to fail. I found this out after the first residential treatment program. I may have stayed clean for the duration of the program, but when I went home, I did not put what I learned into practice.

I have spent time at Women's Own Detox a total of eight times.

Chapter Four

I was seven months pregnant during one of my many stays at detox. That was a trip in itself, mostly because I wasn't allowed to have my own room on the "house" side because there was concern for the baby. I had to sleep or curl my big-bellied body on a wooden cushion seat. It was very uncomfortable.

In my time in recovery, I have attended many sobriety programs. I've had many counselors, therapists, psychologists, healers, and helpers, all designed to aid in my journey of recovery. Today, fourteen years later, I still attend programs, even though I run my own programs.

Upon coming out of treatment for the second time, I moved in with my sister and her family until I was able to find my own place. I attended meetings five days a week, and I was very active in Alcoholics Anonymous. I expected to stay at my sister's for only a short amount of time because I was sure I'd be able to find a place of my own. Of course, "my own place" would be without my children because they were in the care of their father.

It's nothing short of a miracle that I stayed clean during the time spent at my sister's home. Everybody in that house used something, whether it was alcohol, weed, or cocaine. Indeed, I was the only sober person there at any given time. By then, I wanted so desperately to be clean that nothing or nobody was going to stand in my way.

Chapter Five

At this point, I had reestablished a relationship with my former boyfriend Tom, who was a full-blown crack addict. He was in prison at the time, so it just seemed logical for us to be together and start fresh, right? Wrong ... I didn't know any better. I was new to the program and I thought that, if I allowed Tom to smoke his weed and drink, he would not want to smoke crack. It worked! But not for long.

I'd clearly forgotten the contract I'd signed with Kwasi. One day, I came home from work and Tom was not home. I had his kids, but he was nowhere to be found. I called him but he didn't answer. I called and called, and he finally answered. He told me that he was sorry but he'd relapsed.

Naturally I was very pissed off, and slightly triggered, but not enough to join him with a relapse of my own. The fact that he had used wasn't even the worst part. The worst part, I thought, was that he was sneaky about it. In hindsight, I remembered that every relapse I've experienced and heard about definitely included being sneaky and deceptive to loved ones.

I was furious to learn that he took a thousand dollars from my landlord to fix the roof, which was another thing that I was in the dark about. He took that thousand dollars and it all went up in crack smoke. In his addict logic, dear Tom thought that he could make the money back so, after smoking all the money, he stayed out on the streets, certain that he would recoup the money. Of course he did not.

He came home a week or so later—broken and feeling guilty. He was guilty over what he'd done, and I'm sure he felt the shame over the addict he'd become. I took him back. We talked about what he was going to do differently the next time something triggered him.

The tears flowed from his eyes like a waterfall. He vowed never again. Tom said he was done using. I didn't believe him then and, all these years later, I still don't believe he was telling the truth. My reluctance to trust his "never again" words was confirmed only days later when Tom betrayed me and his recovery once again. Yes, folks, he went back out. And this time, Tom ended up in jail. Our relationship died a painful death in June 2006.

By the time Tom went to jail, the seed of using was already planted in my mind. You see, when people who are in recovery relapse, it's not something that happens in a blink of an eye. It's a process that usually begins emotionally and/or psychologically. If it's not addressed, then the actual picking up of the drug is inevitable. The use itself is the last part of the relapse. A relapse can start months before the actual act of using. This is why placing yourself in the company of other people who are using—people who constantly talk about using or are involved in some kind of criminal activity—can and often will plant the seed of using.

You see, if you were a stage three addict—one who uses hard core and daily (like myself)—it usually comes with criminal activity. Who am I going to rob? How am I going to get money today? Getting drugs and preparing drugs and using them is a full-time job.

So Tom's relapse had already planted the seed in me and, unfortunately, I relapsed at the end of August. Just thinking about the steps that I took to get the drugs and use the drugs, and the insanity that went with it, is causing anxiety in me as I write this down. However, it happened and three things happened during that terrible time.

1. I allowed drug users and drug dealers in my home,
2. I allowed my son and his friends to stay in my place and do a lot of Bandola (crimes), and
3. I met the love of my life.

Chapter Six

I met Adrian during a rough time in my life. I had just relapsed a few weeks before. A mutual friend introduced us. I was trying to stop using but—if you know anything about addiction, especially crack—you don't just stop once you start. We talked on the phone a bit and he visited me a few times, as well. I neglected to tell Adrian that I had a drug and alcohol problem until we went out a couple of times. The first time we went out, we went to dinner and then I took him to Cheers on the Danforth. I got drunk pretty quickly and almost fell on the dance floor, but I didn't think I felt the need to tell him at that time. So I'm not sure it was an indication of drunkenness or loyalty to myself, I guess I would say both.

The last time we went out drinking was somewhere in Scarborough. We went to a Chinese restaurant that had a pool table. We played a few games of pool and listened to music all night. So, while we were having a great time, I still felt the need to order two beers and two shots with every round—and there were many. I can't really remember much because I was drinking out of control. Adrian said he only had a couple. Unbeknownst to me, because I was having a fabulous time, the owner of the restaurant called Adrian over and told him that I was cut off and was not going to be served any more alcohol. I was blissfully unaware, because I'm sure if I'd have known at the time, I would have caused havoc. Adrian told me afterwards.

I guess the owner was scared because I'd consumed so much alcohol, he felt the need to cut me off. Now I wasn't argumentative. I wasn't cursing or loud or anything. I just drank too much in this person's eyes. I vaguely remember that night. Just little snippets here and there, but I had a great time. I don't know why, but that night, I decided to tell him that I was actually a person with a chemical dependency. I knew that, with my addiction, he and I would never last.

I didn't want to be that "raging druggie" or alcoholic with him. I had no idea where this was going to go. To tell you the truth, I didn't think it was going to go anywhere. I thought we would've shared a few "hit and runs," and then go our separate ways.

My real fear was that I would fall back into the drugs, which wouldn't have taken much. I really didn't want that, whether I was with him or somebody else. I felt this way because the battle was still going on within me. So I told him.

This was my first time showing some accountability for myself and my actions with someone else, who I didn't even know, and didn't have to share my story with. I was kind of fearful when I told him, because I knew that, once I told him, he might not want to be with me under those circumstances.

Chapter Seven

I remember during those early sober days, I thought I could sell weed and keep my "regulars" around without being compromised. Clearly, I was still very sick. My niece stole some of the weed from me, leaving me in debt and compromised. I fronted that weed from a friend. To this day I owe him that money. It was a lot of weed.

I need to pay him back because that is part of the process of recovering and keeping sobriety. Being accountable and responsible for my actions, even after 14 years of sobriety is required. I still need to make amends.

As for my "regulars," that didn't last long at all. I couldn't participate in that lifestyle without indulging in some kind of chemical or alcohol influence. I felt undervalued, and I certainly was, but it was me who had been choosing to undervalue myself. I was sober and I felt I deserved more than what I was getting.

Part of me still feels the shame of sharing this, but it is the truth. My truth. I was a woman so broken, victimized, and compromised that I had no sense of self-worth. A woman who thinks so little of herself is bound to devalue herself, and that was me in a nutshell. I realized that I was still making poor choices which, unbeknownst to me at the time, were really a reenactment of all the other poor choices.

I had made a choice to stop using, which was the best choice for me. But as I have said and it is worth repeating, it's not just stopping drug use, it's also about the lifestyle. It is necessary to remove the people, places. and things that go along with using drugs on a level three scale which contribute to the continuum of poor choices. You see, although I was sober in the physical sense, I was not sober in the mental and emotional sense.

I finally made a decision to live a clean and sober life, which meant no doing drugs, and no selling. It meant keeping my distance from people in the life of drug use. I surrendered once again on an emotional and mental level, to be one hundred percent in, and I did well… until… I relapsed a year later.

During my sober time before that big destructive and last relapse, life was okay. I say it was okay because I was behaving as if I were a toddler. I was relearning to live.

Chapter Eight

Friday evenings were difficult. I would lay on the couch and do nothing. My mind would wander back to the times when the girls and I were getting ready to go out. I would start with a beer and a couple pills before getting ready to go party. And then I would distance myself from my girls, so I could really dive into the drugs.

Now, I was beyond bored. I had to find things to do with myself.

I was building a new relationship with my children. And I was building a relationship with Adrian. We met in September 2006 and moved in together in December. He asked me to marry him that same month.

It was very hard. I went to twelve-step meetings and I was working my steps…and I had a sponsor. I was doing what I was supposed to do. I was building relationships anew in every area of my life.

I am a person who loves music and loves to go dancing. I have always loved dancing, starting from my teenage years. It was not encouraged for people like me, who was new in recovery. But dancing was something that I needed to do because I loved it.

I remember Adrian taking me to my first mansion party and I was so uncomfortable. First, because I knew nobody there. Second, because the drinks were flowing. The place was packed and you could barely move. If I turned in any direction, there were people around me with drinks in their hands. I don't know how I managed to stay sober and still attend functions, but by then, I wanted sobriety more than I wanted to drink.

So that first year was busy. I dedicated myself wholly to my recovery. I did everything that was suggested of me, and I was practicing the principles in all my affairs. I did everything I could to ensure my sobriety.

It wasn't easy. I was still very sick mentally and I still had all of my old behaviors and defects of character. Those behaviors certainly came to the surface when I was agitated, or if I felt that I was wronged … sometimes they came to the surface just because I was waking up.

You have to understand that I had been using crack cocaine since I was seventeen years old. And before that, I was drunk. My mental capacity was really that of a teenager because, using substances at a young age stunts your mental and emotional growth. In short: you just don't move beyond the age you were when you began using.

You can't just change your normal balance with chemical substances especially when you have used drugs and alcohol for decades. So in the first year, I found myself questioning everything, including this new relationship that I just entered.

Adrian was stepping away from his past and I was stepping away from mine, and we both had control issues. Maybe it wasn't control issues as much as it was refusing to take any shit.

If Adrian said something that I didn't like, or vice versa, we would lock horns. It was an exercise in frustration and it was extremely challenging.

Chapter Nine

A short time after my first year of continuous sobriety, we were invited to a party at my sister's home. I told myself that I would have a drink at her party to celebrate my one year of sobriety. Do you see how the insanity of this disease screws up all logic?

It was just preposterous to think that I could drink after I celebrated my first year of sobriety.

Clearly my head was not right. I had done some of the footwork, but I had not truly surrendered.

The seed was planted months before I relapsed, and it was indeed a nasty affair. On the eve of my relapse, I had convinced myself that taking a couple of Valium would help calm my nerves, which were rattled due to several incidents I'd had with my two oldest children. The next night my addiction convinced me again to take four more, and that was it.

Adrian came home to a woman wearing sexy lingerie. I'd prepared dinner for him. At this point, the wall was holding me up, but oh well. From my point of view, I had done a loving thing by cooking my man dinner and putting on a sexy negligée. You know how they do it in the movies.

However, this wasn't a romantic movie. In fact, it was the beginning of what can only be compared to a horror flick. As soon as Adrian opened the door, I sauntered over to greet him. I thought I was sexy as hell. I was happy to see him and thought he would be happy to see me. Why wouldn't he? I mean, his sexy woman had cooked a meal for him.

However, he immediately saw that I was high. My lover was clearly upset and he let me know it in no uncertain terms. This, of course, made me upset, so I said what I normally say when my back is against the wall or I'm feeling ashamed. I said fuck it.

I took off my engagement ring—thank God because I'm sure I would've sold it. I got dressed, grabbed my purse, and out the door I went. I was on a mission to find my drug of choice and it turned into a horrific 21-day nightmare of drugs and alcohol.

It was a purely insane relapse. After the 21 days of hell, I wanted to die. When I came to, I was vibrating. I looked like shit and felt like shit. My body was screaming for more drugs, but by some kind of miracle I fought back and, with brute strength, I was victorious over my addiction.

I spent Christmas Day dinner with my mom, my kids and my ex-husband. I did sneak a drink just to calm my nerves down, which it did, but of course my addiction whispered in my ear to make a plan to go use when we got downtown. Thankfully my Creator intervened.

That night, I walked into my aunt's house having nowhere else to go, since I clearly couldn't return to the home I shared with Adrian. I called him and he shared what this experience had done to him. I was on an emotional rollercoaster.

I had a mixed bag of emotions that included fear, anxiety, and of course, my old friend, shame. My whole world had been flipped upside down and I didn't know if I was coming or going. I didn't know where I was going to live. I didn't know anything.

Adrian and I planned for me to go home the next day so we could talk. The pain I had caused him was catastrophic, and not good for his mental wellbeing. I felt so guilty for what I'd done to him and was so full of shame for the monster that I believed I was. I just wanted the world to swallow me up.

Adrian and I spoke through wracking sobs, and I, once again, made promises that I wasn't sure that I was capable of keeping. Yet, this time it was not a lie. This time, I meant every word of those promises.

I slept in the spare bedroom for a while, because Adrian wasn't ready to have me back in our bed. Even though it hurt, I understood. This was the beginning of my one hundred percent surrender to my Creator, and so began the healing.

Chapter Ten

As I have said many times, sobriety is not just about the end of using the chemical, or mood-altering substances. It's so much more.

It's looking at my part in darkness I'd not only caused myself pain, but my loved ones as well. It was now time for me to start looking at the little girl in me who was suffering. I had to come to terms and except that I wasn't raised by my biological parents. I had to acknowledge out loud that my so-called family member had molested me at the tender age of eleven.

I had to look at all of my physical, sexual, mental, and emotional abuse. I had to look at everything including those who I hurt. So, besides working the Twelve Steps of Narcotics Anonymous, I needed to seek help for my trauma.

I went to the WRAP program, which is a program for women recovering from abuse at Women's College Hospital. Fortunately for me, I only had to wait a few months to get in, because I had already experienced some form of recovery with umpteen counseling sessions. I wasn't new.

I had to go to the pre-intensive phase, which was an expectation of everybody, twice weekly, in the evenings. The reason for the pre-intensive sessions was to gauge your level of commitment, so you were not taking a spot from someone who was devoted to improving their situation. I wanted this more than I ever wanted anything.

It wasn't that long before I was accepted into the fall program, which was every day for four months—Monday through Friday, from nine until one pm. I was nothing if not dedicated to following the program. I lived in Scarborough at the time, so I had to get up early every day and make my way downtown.

I enjoyed the program although, being my rebellious self, I had to challenge the counselors. At the time, I believed I already knew everything, which can easily make a person unteachable. When I was asked to share, I did so with graphic detail. I shared about having been raped and sodomized. But when it came to me giving my personal account of the physical and sexual abuse I had endured, the counselors would stop me. Apparently, I wasn't feeling the emotions of the trauma. They wanted me to experience those emotions rather than simply recite the events. It was clear to them that I was still numbing my feelings, even though I wasn't using drugs and alcohol.

It upset me when they would stifle my recital in mid-sentence, or before I was finished. At the time, I didn't understand the process that they were trying to show me. They wanted me to get in touch with my body. That took some time.

I learned a lot from that program and I was able to let go of a lot once I finally surrendered.

Chapter Eleven

It was two weeks before I was to graduate from the program and I was so excited to take the tools I'd learned and get to living my best life. Then something happened that, once again, changed the course of my journey.

One morning ,when I was getting up, I received a call from the police telling me that my ex-husband had been arrested and they wanted me to pick up my children. I wasn't going to the program that day because I had my youngest boy, Curtis, and I was taking him to speech therapy. I still thank my Creator that my youngest son did not have to witness the raid. My poor daughters, however, were present and were forced to listen to the cops beat their father.

My niece was also there and the children were more than shaken by the experience. My daughter later told me that the police turned up the TV so they couldn't hear their daddy getting beat. By then, Kwasi was screaming out to them.

Just remembering those words from my daughter's mouth still shakes me up today. Not because my ex-husband got beaten but because my children were there and were exposed to the brutality. I can still recall my daughter, Celeste, telling me that the only thing that she asked the police was if she could take her new shoes with her because she was graduating, and thankfully, they let her take her shoes.

So within a matter of hours the three kids were with Adrian and me in a two-bedroom apartment. That transition was a very difficult adjustment for everybody involved. You see, the kids were not in my care for a couple of years because of my addiction and, although Adrian had children of his own and had them live with us at different periods of their lives, Adrian didn't know my kids and they didn't know him.

Their young lives, once again, went through an upheaval because of their father and me. It was challenging to say the least. Adrian had his ways of living and structure, and the kids were coming from a home that had no structure. I just wanted to fix everything. It was a formidable time.

There were plenty of disagreements between Adrian and I regarding how he dealt with my children. For me to describe it, I would have to say that I felt like I was a battered woman with an alcoholic husband and scared children. Don't get me wrong, that is not how it was by any means, but I felt I was tippy toeing around to make sure that the kids didn't do anything to upset Adrian, who has OCD.

So now my children, who didn't clean up after themselves when they lived with their father, had been dropped into a completely different way of living. I can tell you that it caused plenty of animosity. After a couple of years, my children and I moved out. If we didn't move when we did, I don't think Adrian and I would be together today.

No matter what, I had to protect my children and I did. They had been through quite enough in their young lives and now it was time for me to step up and be a mother. I was fiercely protective. Mothers know how it is.

I didn't like the expectation that they were to immediately adjust to another man's way of doing things.

I guess what it boils down to is that, I don't know why but, every time Adrian tried to positively discipline them, I felt something rip inside of me, not unlike a mamma bear. So to preserve my relationship with both Adrian and my children, I got on the list for Native Housing and, because of the circumstances, I was able to get on as a priority.

Chapter Twelve

Within a year, I got my three-bedroom house. I was so happy and so scared at the same time. I had never in my life lived alone. Since I moved out of my mother's house at the age of fifteen, I have always lived with somebody. Of course, the kids are somebody, but I had to take charge and protect them. So it was different. And even though the people I lived with had not been able to protect me, I still felt safer with another adult in the home. So you can imagine the transition for me was brutal.

The first week I slept in the living room because I feared that someone was going to come through the front window or through the back door. It was scary, but it was so good to be sober and back with my babies. Moving into my new home with my children was one of the greatest gifts I could have received.

But the transition was a daily challenge. My children each had a different personality, which was quite difficult for all of us. Added to the mixed bag of personalities, there was the trauma that each child had suffered at the hands of my drug use and their father's actions.

The trauma ran deep for all of us, but I was an adult and they were children, so I had to step up and help them. So not only did I have to deal with the daily battle to keep my addiction from becoming active, it was also up to me to help my children deal with the trauma caused by their parents.

Most of all, I had to constantly reassure my children. They had to trust that I wouldn't walk away and activate my addiction. If I did, it meant that I would, again, walk away from them. I'm glad that I had my children because it forced me to get up every day and work my recovery program one day at a time. I knew I couldn't vow to them that I would never use drugs again because it's an impossible promise to make. A person who works an honest program knows that each day is but a daily reprieve and tomorrow is not a promise they can make where recovery is concerned.

The only promise I could make was that I would do everything in my power to not fall prey to negative outer influence or the inner pain of my once shattered soul. Addiction is cunning, baffling, and powerful, so resting on my laurels was not then, and is not now, an option.

Chapter Thirteen

It was such a thrill for me to decorate this three-bedroom house and make it our home. We also had a big basement, and a massive back yard. But it was a conundrum. For the ten years I lived there, I could do nothing with the back yard. The kids' schools were not even five minutes from the house which was perfect. There was a public school and right beside it was junior high and the kids were settling into a nice routine.

During this time, I allowed my oldest daughter to come and live with us. I had helped her escape an abusive relationship that produced a child. I was so happy—over the moon—at the prospect of having her come live with us. I wanted so badly to make up for not being able to raise her. I wanted to correct all of those lies that were said to her about me.

There's an unsavory truth involved and as painful as it was to admit things, I wanted to be one hundred percent honest with her. After all the years of my drug-fueled absence, did she not deserve to know the truth? So I told her my truth. But my confession was the polar opposite of what she was told by others.

It completely blows my mind when I think about what was done to her. Because how could anybody say that they love me, and tear me down to my daughter. People told her that I never wanted her. That is the cruelest thing that you could do to a child.

It was unbelievably painful for me to find out that this was a lie she had been raised on, and it was even more painful for my daughter to hear my words.

I don't think that I will ever forgive those people. Although I had my part in her pain, I believe this caused the biggest part, because they destroyed any forgiveness that my daughter might have had in her heart. My mom's constant negative talk about me hindered or maybe even frightened her to want to forgive me. She may have felt that she would be betraying my mom in some way if she did. Fear can breed wickedness and I'm positive that fear was the driving force behind their betrayal.

I was so excited when my oldest daughter came to live with us, because me and my kids would finally be a family under the same roof. At the time, I was blissfully unaware that she was harboring a deep and bitter resentment towards me.

The truth is, I cannot speak for her and I can only imagine her jealousy when it came to the other three who had the benefit of being, for the most part, raised by me. She had no way of knowing my ways of disciplining my kids. It got real ugly with us at the worst time.

Chapter Fourteen

My son Cameron and his girlfriend Alyssa were blessed with a beautiful baby boy named Camari. This little baby was born on his father's birthday. Can you imagine a better birthday gift for a man than a baby boy? Unfortunately this amazing gift turned into the deepest loss for my family:

Sweet, beautiful Camari passed away at two days old. The devastation, confusion, and shock were palpable. There were so many particulars and questions surrounding Camari's passing. How? Why? What did they do? What didn't they do? Ultimately an autopsy revealed that my sweet grandchild had pneumonia and meningitis.

But we had unanswered questions and I lay blame at the feet of the hospital staff. They encouraged, or should I say *coerced* Cameron and Alyssa to cremate Camari so quickly that we couldn't order our own autopsy. The hospital robbed our family of our peace of mind and we are still in the dark about the real cause of Camari's passing. It's a loss that we all feel and we always will, but it is the worst for Cameron and Alyssa. Alyssa has grieved and continues to grieve but my son, as far as I know, still has not allowed himself to.

Unfortunately because of my active addiction, Cameron and I are not close. This is a sadness that will stay with me always. However, as long as I am living and staying clean, hope remains that we will bridge the cavernous gap that lies between us. I will always hold out hope that our relationship will improve.

After my grandson's memorial, everybody came back to my house to celebrate the baby and his too short life. I heard from the other children that my oldest daughter was angry that I had bought Cameron clothing more conducive to attending a funeral. I did this due to the fact that Cameron's usual attire is Nikes, baggy pants, and hoodies. I didn't want him wearing such casual clothes to his son's funeral, so I bought him some slacks, shoes, and a nice shirt.

For my eldest daughter this was a cardinal sin. One of my friends overheard her and her sidekick at the time talking bad about me. My girlfriend asked why she was saying those things about me and told her that I was doing the best that I could. I'm still trying to wrap my head around that incident, but I digress.

It is known that hurt people hurt people. After the celebration of life, I went to bed and I started feeling ill that night. Probably my body was just rundown, but I started feeling sick. When I woke up the next day, I was not feeling well at all. My young son, Curtis, came into my room and told me there was cheese in the fridge, and asked if he could have some.

Of course, I said yes. My daughter, however, was having none of this and she started screaming. She bought the cheese. She didn't want Curtis to have any. I jumped out of bed and ran downstairs to find out what her problem was. After all, it's only cheese. Clearly the cheese had nothing to do with her outburst.

She kept flapping her mouth and getting in my face, and then she pushed me. Exhausted and angry, I grabbed her and pinned her against the wall, which I am not proud of. My other two daughters, Celeste and Cheyenne, stepped in and broke up the shoving match. Their sister, however, hell bent on continuing, grabbed my vacuum cleaner and whipped it on the ground. I ran up to her and we were screaming at each other and then, all of a sudden, my first-born daughter punched me in my face.

I couldn't believe she did that and, in a split second, I grabbed her and I was ready to put a beating on her. Thank God, I remembered that she was pregnant, which she'd clearly forgotten, or maybe she simply didn't care. Once again, the girls stopped it from escalating.

I called her a little bitch and told her to get out of my house. She left and we haven't spoken since. That was twelve years ago.

Chapter Fifteen

Since that fateful day, my oldest daughter has assassinated my character in so many ways and in the most disgusting manner. She has vilified me on social media. She and her sidekick posted that I had beat her when she was a little girl.

The truth is, I never raised a finger to her as a child or ever before this incident. And she claims that she was not the only one on the receiving end of my wrath. According to her, her siblings were also beaten by me. My daughter's accusations are pure fabrication brought on by her bitter resentment.

My mom hardly ever allowed me to be alone with her. My daughter tells anyone who will listen that I put needles in my arms which is another lie. The truth is that even at my worst and lowest point of active addiction, I never used drugs intravenously. This defamation of character is as repugnant as it is untrue.

Only a person seething with bitter animosity and anger would say those things about her own mother. I mean, even if there was an ounce of truth to it, what kind of person talks about her mother like that? My daughter seems to delight in depreciating me as a person using any platform she can, as long as it's in a public arena. She even went as far as to go to my workplace and tell them rotten slanderous lies to get me fired. I ask you, what kind of person does this?

The short answer? Someone who needs help to navigate her feelings. My heart hurts for us both.

Chapter Sixteen

Despite all of the nasty and hurtful things that have been said about me by my own blood, no less, I can still find joy in the fact that I remain steadfast in my recovery. No matter what has been done to me, I have the pure pleasure of waking up clean and sober each morning.

Another incident that was a blow to my recovery was when I sat down with my parents and read a letter to them. The letter included my sexual abuse at the hands of one of their own. I can't tell you what it took for me after thirty years to share those words with them, and I received no validation. Every friend that I have ever had knows this incident to be true. Why would I lie?

Why would I tell all of my friends, at the age of twelve, about something so abominable and disgusting if it wasn't true? I've held onto this for decades. That incident changed the trajectory of my life.

I didn't care about my body, and a couple of years later, I lost my virginity.

In my mind, the only way someone could love me was if I gave my body to him.

I only wanted to be wanted, and I thought that was the only way.

From then on, my body was no longer mine. It was yours, his, theirs; whether I willingly gave it up or it was forcefully taken from me—that was actually a regular occurrence in my days of using.

Because of my mom's denial, I was denied a relationship with her. I was never the same, right up until she passed away. These things that happened to me drove me to do what I do now, which is counsel women and children who have been abused.

If you can just imagine, these incidents occurred around the same time. What happened with my daughter and trying to share this information from my childhood with my parents, which they denied. This is important to me. I was called a liar and not validated ... and yet I still stayed sober.

Because of this incident, I never went back up to my parents' home until one year before Mom passed away. I've had to come to terms with the fact that I will never receive atonement for what my abuser has done to me. He denies it. His sidekick denies it, as if she was there. Another family member questioned me, indicating that she's not accepting of my truth.

So I had to strengthen my sobriety and recovery and just move forward. I know what happened and my Creator knows what happened. Today, I walk with my head held high. The truth is, I can go around to him, get in his face, and kick off; and part of me would also love to do it. My family knows that I could and would do it in a heartbeat but, what's the purpose of doing that really?

They will not take my power again. I have seen that person maybe once or twice if that and not since my mom's funeral. I do not wish to see him ever again but if he ever comes up in front of me, you can believe that the mighty woman I have become, despite what he did to me, will handle it.

On the flipside to that coin is that most of our family members have been sexually assaulted in one form or another, and it's normal for them to sweep it under the rug, pretend it didn't happen or accept it. Shit happens I know. When we were young, we were curious.

We want to touch, and we want to explore our sexuality. I get that because it's a normal part of growing up. However when a teenage boy sexually interferes with a young girl, it's not *curious exploration*. It is *deviant exploitation*.

As much as the little girl inside of me wants the monster to suffer and pay for what he did, the grown woman that I have become—who has made many mistakes in life—forgives him. It's as simple as that. Just writing these words and remembering blows my mind that I stayed sober for such a long time. But I have. Maybe not gracefully, but I have.

Chapter Seventeen

As I continued to settle into our home, I decided my next move in life would be to go to college. I knew it was something I truly wanted and yet I was terrified. Seeds of doubt haunted me and questions danced in my brain. Was I smart enough? Would the fear of not being able to do it cause me to give up? Would I self-sabotage my future success?

Despite these questions, I forged on and began the preparation to become an adult student. My chosen field is advocacy for and counselling of abused women and children. It took three years to do it, but I succeeded.

Prior to and during the years I spent in school I continually had stomach issues, mostly diarrhea. My ass seemed to be on fire most of the time. I just chalked it up to all the alcohol I drank in the past and maybe whatever I was eating. But the pain became so bad that I had a couple of colonoscopies. They found nothing.

At some point, they told me I have gastritis and a little bit of pancreatitis. But I knew it was more than that. I would go for lunch after class and I would eat something. Then I would be in agonizing pain for the rest of the day, never knowing why. Finally, I found another doctor, and he discovered I had Crohn's disease. Twenty centimeters of my bowels were diseased.

I was losing weight, which seemed awesome at first. However, I kept losing weight and I wasn't looking good. I was looking sick. Then I was diagnosed with narrow angles and eye disease plus Anklosing spondylitis. My back or my spine was fusing together. All three were connected.

I already knew I had to start wearing glasses and get surgery on my eyes and I'm thinking, "What is going on?"

As my Crohn's disease progressed, I had one course left to do before I graduated from college. Unfortunately, I had to put a halt to going to school. The doctors were giving me infusions and, for the six weeks, they were not working. The diseased bowel had to be removed. They told me it would be an easy laparoscopic procedure. That I would be in and out with no problem.

But when Adrian, who was now my hubby, arrived to pick me up at the appointed time, he was told it would be longer because when they began the laparoscopic surgery, they realized there was a lot more bowel disease than they first thought. They had to stop, and instead go up and down my body thirty-five centimeters long.

The diseased bowel was a lot longer than they anticipated. Adrian was terrified.

When I came out of surgery I was stapled from top to bottom. It was a brutal surgery and even more challenging was the adjustment to what accompanies a surgery like that.

I have to live a certain way for the rest of my life and it doesn't even guarantee that the problem won't come back. After my surgery, however, I did the last course I needed to graduate and I passed. I even can't tell you the tears and the joy that came from such an accomplishment.

I dedicated all of this to my mother Glenda. Her life was cut short and I blame my grandmother for my mother's suffering. So this was for her, to let her know that she didn't die in vain.

As long as I have breath in me, so does my mother and father. I remember the day of the commencement. I had a severe

Crohn's outbreak, which attacked my eyes and under my eyes. Underneath my eyes, there was swelling and crustaceans. It was quite nasty but it didn't stop me.

I covered what I could, which didn't help much because the glasses I had on magnified everything. Yet, I put that gown on and I walked with people who I had not studied with because I had stopped my studies due to my illness. When the moment came, when I walked up to the podium and received my diploma—the only way I can describe that feeling is pure love and second to none respect for myself. It was an amazing gift to overcome all those adversities in my life. I can tell you, I felt immense pride.

Chapter Eighteen

I have received so many gifts since getting sober and I've met so many amazing people in the rooms of many twelve step groups, such as Alcoholic and Cocaine Anonymous. These people mean the world to me because they've walked the same path of active addiction as I have. These people understand what I went through in active addiction and what challenges I face in recovery.

I met a woman who I call Aunt Cindy in the rooms. Aunt Cindy knew my mother Glenda from the days when she dated Cindy's brother. I believe mom lived at her nanny's house, which was very close.

I've met countless people through my journey, many of whom knew both my mom, Glenda, and my father, Kirtus. I've had the pleasure of spending time with people who shared stories of both of them, good and bad.

I lost a woman who meant the world to me. She was like a mother to me. Aunt Janet left an imprint on my heart as well as a void in my soul.

On my journey, I have found so many of the Gabriel side of my family and, today, I have relationships with them. It's a huge family indeed.

My commitment to my recovery, and my dedication to advocate on behalf of women and children who've been through abject trauma, gives me great pride, and fuels me to move forward every day. I have been working within the indigenous community for a number of years now and I can't tell you how fulfilling it's been. I've actually created my own business: *D. Gabriel Wellbriety Services.* I facilitate healing circles.

I've had the pleasure of speaking alongside a very influential government official, which is an amazing gift indeed. I've been part of many speaking engagements for international recovery day. One of the greatest testaments to my commitment to help others overcome their addiction issues is the fact that I go to prisons to facilitate twelve step programs.

It was such a satisfaction to walk into the prison—without handcuffs—and be able to walk out the front door a short time later. The gratification that comes from one addict helping another is immeasurable.

Chapter Nineteen

A call to service drove me to go to the Don jail and facilitate a meeting for the men. I was part of the Hospitals and Institutions committee for three years. Every year, they would honor us with an amazing dinner and give us a nice pin with the volunteer logo on it and a date marking the years of service.

It's important to be involved in service, whether it's setting up chairs and making coffee for the meetings or larger scale — speaking in prisons, treatment centers, and hospitals. They say you will not be able to keep recovery if you don't give it away. This sounds like an oxymoron but the reality is that service to others is crucial in recovery. When you help others, you also help yourself stay clean.

Active addiction is something I wouldn't wish on my worst enemy. Not that I have foes any more. Today, I surround myself with people who love me. In short, I have given to others what was so freely given to me when I was a newcomer.

I dedicate my life to helping others, but the sad thing is, if you were to ask my children, they would probably say I help others more than I help them (my own family). Maybe there's a sliver of truth to that. However, no matter how willing I am to give, the other person has to be willing to receive. I have always, at least during my years of recovery, been willing to help my children.

On the flipside, my children know that, for many years, I parented through guilt, which allowed them to be inconsiderate, sometimes selfish and lazy. I did everything for them and I found that I was not doing them any favors by spoiling them. Today I can say, until my last breath of air, I will do the best that I can do for my children and grandchildren.

That wasn't always the case. I felt so guilty about them, that I let them get away with things. Now my girls are hard workers and support their children better than I supported them. It could have been worse for them as adults. I could have, through my guilt-fueled mode of parenting, really ruined them.

What I need to do as a mother is let them fall and let them pick themselves up. I want nothing more than for my babies to grow up to be strong self-sufficient people. People who are loving, kind, generous and understanding. Most of all, I wish for them to understand forgiveness. I want them to know that it's okay to receive help.

I, as a mother, don't always have the answers. I may not have always been the best role model, but today, I do the best that I can as a mother and a grandmother, whether my children choose to believe it or not. I have a number of grandchildren but I only have a relationship with three. There are three who I am not able to see because of their mother, my oldest daughter, and her venomous resentment towards me. This is unfortunate, not only for me and my daughter, but also for her children, who don't know their maternal grandmother's love.

I am ever hopeful that one day my oldest daughter and I will build a bridge of love and become one in our family unit. Until that happens, and even if it doesn't, I pray for them each day and night.

I would not be real if I told you recovery was all sunshine and rainbows. The truth is, it can be hard and not always fun, especially for the newcomer. I'd be lying if I told you that, throughout my fifteen years of sobriety, I have never wanted to drink. Of course I have thought about it many times. I even went as far as to park my car in front of a beer store one day, but my friend, Jessie, taught me to "play the tape through to the end." Today, whenever I want a drink, I tell myself, "OK Desnee, so you're going to have a drink. Then what? After you use, you're going to go into your house and sell all of your jewelry. Then all the electronics. The money will surely run out.

Then what?

I am probably going to invite some dealers over to my house. Then what?

I'm probably going to go outside and see who I can rob and this will be after I've cleaned out all of my bank accounts.

Then what?

I run the whole stinking affair through my mind. Until... I am in handcuffs;

Until... I have lost the love of my life.
Until... my children refuse to bring their kids, my beloved grandchildren, around me.
Until... I have lost the love and respect of the ones I have come to love and respect
Until... I am at the point where I no longer want to live.

I don't know where active addiction would take me, in the physical sense, but I know in the emotional sense, it would take me to a place of utter despair. Who in their right mind, after all of that, would still want to use?

With my long list of pure hellish outcomes, I choose to stay clean and sober.

Now it's not easy when the demons are dancing around in your head. When you have family members or people or places that trigger a memory or a feeling. It's not a fun feeling. In fact, it is a very uncomfortable feeling.

I've asked myself why has the Creator given me the gift of sobriety when so many other people in my life have left this earth because of their active addiction. The only answer that comes to my mind is that I am supposed to do what I'm doing, which is trying to help the next suffering addict.

Through my sobriety, I have gone on many vacations. I bought my own vehicle for the first time in my life at the ripe age of forty-eight. Yes, you read that right, my first vehicle.

It's not that I never had the money to buy a car, because I can tell you with certainty, thousands of dollars have passed through my hands. It just never stayed in my hands long enough to buy anything but drugs. It always ended up in a drug dealer's pockets, and I'm also certain that I have put more than one child through college. Sadly it wasn't my child. No, I put my drug dealer's children through college.

Today I have different priorities. I have beautiful grandbabies, so a vehicle has been a very good investment. It's with well-earned pride that I will also say, ``next time I put a child through college, it will be one of my own."

I travel when and where I want to. I can go beyond a world that once crippled me. Because I am clean and sober, I love life, and I live it to the fullest. I have a beautiful loving extended family that I have gained through Adrian, who has been an amazing partner. I love his children as if they were mine. My in-laws are also wonderful. My mother-in-law is so thoughtful and caring and she can throw down in the kitchen. All of them are beautiful people. Even Adrian's exes are fantastic. Yup, you read me right. I have never had an issue with any of them. Well maybe one, but it's okay. We are family. They have accepted me and I them.

Chapter Twenty

Today I take life as it comes. I suffer with an eating disorder called B.E.D, which has plagued me for many years. I am still fighting that fight. It boggles my mind how I can recover from drug/alcohol addiction but I can't surrender to this disorder. It's like I am still finding ways to hurt myself, proving to outsiders and myself that I am not worthy of peace, love, and forgiveness.

It's very common to transfer addictions. I struggle deeply because, not only is this disorder hurting me emotionally, mentally, and spiritually, it's killing me slowly physically. The inflammation caused by the disorder is wreaking havoc on my Crohn's disease. But do I stop? No. But if you know me well, you will know I will never stop fighting.

I have amazing days when I don't have a care in the world and other days, I am sobbing and feeling pain deep in my soul. On the latter days, I reach out to any and all supports who can yank me from the edge of sanity.

My life hasn't been easy and I sometimes feel cheated after all these years. It's a strange feeling to miss something you have never had, but I miss a life free of monsters. I get sad and I get angry, but I also feel joy that brings forth laughter and dancing, because my addiction is part of me, it does not define me. I try hard not to take things for granted but I also know that I am not perfect, and I will falter at times.

My personality is one of abandoned inhibition and innate caution. Another part of me is quiet, lacking confidence in my abilities. My indigenous spirit name is Circling Wind and my clan is Deer. Given my mixed bag of character flaws and assets, it makes perfect sense that I have such a name.

I guess you could say I am a contradiction personified when it comes to my complex temperament. It's not far-fetched to wonder that maybe I have more than one personality.

Do I wish that my childhood had been different? Absolutely.

Do I wish that I had found different ways of coping with things that have happened to me? Definitely.

The reality is, these things happened and my way of dealing with the trauma was less than stellar. However, the past cannot be changed so I have come to a place of acceptance. I acknowledge my past and, although I am not guilty of the crimes against me, I am one hundred percent accountable for my part.

I have atoned for as much as I can or remember. Most days I love my life, and even the days that I don't—when I'm struggling—I still strive to find gratitude in my heart. It's a matter of making the choice to look for it. I have so many people in my life today who I know love me, and yes, there have been times that I have taken them for granted and truly regret it.

I am constantly trying to better myself even though there are times I feel that I just can't get out of my own way. I do lean towards self-sabotage.

I love my family and, even though there is still some unresolved pain towards some of them, I'll be damned if that pain is going to stop me from reaching for my best life. My hope for my future is peace, acceptance, continuous, understanding, and forgiveness toward myself and others. My greatest desire is to experience, and be surrounded by, love and laughter.

My wish for my children—my three bonus children through love, my life partner and everyone else—is to be kind and gentle to yourself most of all. I believe when you practice kindness towards yourself, it will soon come naturally to pass it on to others.

We all make mistakes, though I can only speak for myself. What I know with one hundred percent certainly, is that I come from generational trauma. Because of that trauma, my children and grandchildren have also experienced it. I am the first generation to break those chains. I am breaking the cycle and, although I tore my world apart as well as my children's, before I began the healing, I am constantly improving. I can only do the best that I can do with what I have right now.

My children will know that they mean the world to me. They will know that I will never stop seeking their forgiveness by showing them respect and teaching them forgiveness through my own examples. Though I cannot take away their pain, I want them to know that I would give anything if I could.

What I can do, however, is show them, through my own actions that, no matter what and despite all adversity, they can rise above anything in their way. That is a gift that is worth more than all the gold in the world. My prayer for those who are lost and suffering is that you find and create a support system for yourself. I encourage you to be around those who will lift you up, or at the very least, avoid those who would tear you down.

We cannot rise without help from others. Many have tried, and that includes me. Together all of us can rise.

As long as I continue to do better, I will be better. I will continue to help those who need it. I will continue to bring my Wellbriety Program wherever I can.

All I want in life is to dance—figuratively and metaphorically— like no one is watching. I want to travel more. I want to experience all I can. I want to continue to forgive myself for what I didn't know and wasn't taught … and to move forward.

*****

This is my life story. I wrote this books to hopefully empower someone. I want my readers to walk away with a better understanding of powerlessness, a better understanding of family trauma (and dynamics), and the re-building of one's personal and hand-me-down dysfunction. You must remember, I wasn't born this way. This was passed down to me. I now hold the torch of surrender. I now pass that healing on to my babies.

****

Review Requested:

We'd like to know if you enjoyed the book.
Please consider leaving a review on the platform
from which you purchased the book.

CPSIA information can be obtained
at www.ICGtesting.com
Printed in the USA
BVHW042044031222
653392BV00001B/2